Smart Guide™

to

Boosting Your Energy

About Smart Guides™

Welcome to Smart Guides. Each Smart Guide is created as a written conversation with a learned friend; a skilled and knowledgeable author guides you through the basics of the subject, selecting the most important points and skipping over anything that's not essential. Along the way, you'll also find smart inside tips and strategies that distinguish this from other books on the topic.

Within each chapter you'll find a number of recurring features to help you find your way through the information and put it to work for you. Here are the user-friendly elements you'll encounter and what they mean:

The Keys

Each chapter opens by highlighting in overview style the most important concepts in the pages that follow.

Smart Move

Here's where you will learn opinions and recommendations from experts and professionals in the field.

Street Smarts

This feature presents smart ways in which people have dealt with related issues and shares their secrets for success.

Smart Sources

Each of these sidebars points the way to more and authoritative information on the topic, from organizations, corporations, publications, Web sites, and more.

Smart Definition

Terminology and key concepts essential to your mastering the subject matter are clearly explained in this feature.

F.Y.I.

Related facts, statistics, and quick points of interest are noted here.

What Matters, What Doesn't

Part of learning something new involves distinguishing the most relevant information from conventional wisdom or myth. This feature helps focus your attention on what really matters.

The Bottom Line

The conclusion to each chapter, here is where the lessons learned in each section are summarized so you can revisit the most essential information of the text.

One of the main objectives of the *Smart Guide to Boosting Your Energy* is to better inform you not only about how energy is created but also about how you can manufacture additional energy for yourself.

Smart Guide™

to

Boosting Your Energy

Nancy Monson

CADER BOOKS

John Wiley & Sons, Inc.

New York • Chichester • Weinheim • Brisbane • Singapore • Toronto

The information contained in this book is not intended to serve as a replacement for professional medical advice. Any use of the information in this book is at the reader's discretion. The author and the publisher specifically disclaim any and all liability arising directly or indirectly from the use or application of any information contained in this book. A health-care professional should be consulted regarding your specific situation.

Grafteful acknowledgment is made for permission to reprint the following: Optimism/pessimism self-assessment quiz (page 19): from M. F. Scheier, C. S. Carver, and M. W. Bridges, "Revised Life Orientation Test (LOT-R)," *Journal of Personality and Social Psychology*, vol. 67, 1994, p. 1073; copyright American Psychological Association; reprinted with permission. Brain dominance self-assessment quiz (pages 22–25) used with permission of Ann McGee-Cooper and Associates, Inc., (e-mail: ann@amac.com). "The Lark & Owl Test" (self-assessment quiz on pages 28–29) copyright 1998 Circadian Technologies, Inc. (Cambridge, MA), from www.circadian.com/learning_center. "Adults and Physical Activity" (page 83), from Centers for Disease Control and Prevention 1992 Behavioral Risk Factor Survey. "Examples of Moderate Amounts of Activity" (page 85), from At-A-Glance companion document to *Physical Activity and Health: A Report of the Surgeon General*, Centers for Disease Control and Prevention.

ISBN 0-471-31859-0

Printed in the United States of America

10 9 8 7 6 5 4 3 2 1

Contents

Introduction

I've often been told that I'm a high-energy person. The big joke in my family has been that you'll come into my house and, as a quilter and crafter, I'll show you what I've accomplished: "I made this and this and this, that and this and that one, this and that one over there. And then on Tuesday, I made this . . ."

Where do I find so much energy? In part, I was born with it. But I also know that my energy comes and goes depending on how well I take care of myself. And, like everyone else, I'm prone to severe energy droughts. (In fact, writing this book has left me exhausted!)

The good news is that I've learned some secrets to life-long zip while researching the *Smart Guide to Boosting Your Energy,* and I'm ready and eager to share them with you. They're actually really very basic, though some might be thought time-consuming. But then, you're smart enough to know that a higher level of energy won't come overnight, or in a magic potion or a pill. You know you're going to have to put in some effort and make some changes. But I've tried to make my recommendations practical and doable. No jargon, no jive. Just good, commonsense advice—and some cutting-edge news, too.

In chapter 1, you will discover the energy basics—how your mind and body interact to create energy, the different types of energy that can be attained (calm is good, tense is bad), and how energy ebbs and flows from hour to hour and day to day.

In chapter 2, you'll have the opportunity to develop your very own energy profile (yes, we're talking quizzes!). After all, to boost your energy level you first have to identify what gives you energy and what takes it away.

Chapter 3 will give you a cursory review of the psychological and physical conditions that can sap energy (stress, depression, and anxiety, as well as sleep deprivation, thyroid disorders, obesity, and iron-deficiency anemia, among others). These energy-robbing problems must be treated—or there's little chance you'll make headway in boosting your zip with the techniques in this book.

Chapters 4 and 5 will arm you with the nutrition and exercise knowledge you need to optimally fuel your body and mind. There's lots of commonsense advice to be found here, as well as the latest thinking about food and activity. Chapter 6 offers a slew of lifestyle strategies for creating energy—from getting more and better rest to turning off the world whenever possible and using music and meditation to rejuvenate.

Chapter 7 gives you the skinny on vitamin, mineral, and herb supplements—the hottest nutritional products on the market. Some of these products really do boost zip, others are just highly touted. Finally, chapter 8 provides a glimpse of some of the more "out there" energy fixes—and warns you about some remedies to avoid. The appendix to the book provides some spot boosters to quickly get you going when your get-up-and-go has got up and left.

Writing this guide has been an educational experience for me. I've learned how to boost my pep not just with candy bars and caffeine but with proper food, activity, rest, and relaxation (as well as some ginseng now and then). My hope is that you, too, will benefit from what I've learned. So read on, and get ready to boost your energy!

CHAPTER 1

·······················

Energy Basics

THE KEYS

• Learn how nature and nurture combine to create your individual energy level.

• Find out how your mind, body, and spirit affect your energy level.

• Determine where your energy level naturally peaks and dips during the course of a day.

• Identify the major differences between calm energy and tense energy.

• Studying how different cultures view the concept of energy gives you options and tools for enhancing your life.

Energy. Vim. Vigor. Vitality. Pep. Kick Zip. Zoom. Oomph. Everybody wants it. Few of us have as much of it as we'd sometimes like. In fact, a lack of energy is an all-too-common complaint among Americans across all ages, genders, and occupations. Surveys suggest that on any one day, a quarter of all people will complain of fatigue.

Is that any wonder, given the demands of modern life? We now live in a global, twenty-four-hour culture, and thanks to beepers, fax machines, e-mail, and answering machines, it's impossible to escape from our responsibilities. Between work, home, family, and societal pressures, there's little time for us to recharge our batteries and find the core of energy that resides inside us.

The good news is that the secret to getting and keeping energy is actually very basic. We all can learn how to boost our energy levels so we can better meet the demands of everyday life. There are even effective ways to preserve vim and vigor as we age. All it takes is just some effort (read energy) directed at your most important source of oomph: you.

What Is Energy?

When you think of energy, the word *vitality* probably comes to mind. You envision people who have a zest for life, a curiosity about the world, and an ability to perform a wide array of physical, intellectual, and emotional tasks without the need to catch their breaths. People with high energy levels have a tremendous capacity to get things accomplished—and to know how to enjoy life. They have the stamina—and the motivation—to keep going when ordinary mortals poop out. They're enthusiastic, and their enthusiasm is often contagious and irresistible. High-energy people seem to have it all—and to be able to do it all, too. Take actor and comedian Robin Williams. He has energy to spare: he exudes vitality, zip, and a love for life. His mind and body operate at a lightning-fast pace, and he always seems to have a bounce in his step and a smile on his face (no matter the ups and downs of his career). Robin can always crack a joke—at himself and the world—and be able to find humor in any situation.

But not all high-energy types are boisterous cheerleaders like Robin Williams. Some have a quiet, centered sort of oomph that is just as contagious. These people, says Ann McGee-Cooper, a business consultant and coauthor of *You Don't Have to Go Home from Work Exhausted!*, don't need to shout their enthusiasm for their energy to be felt by others. Their vital spark shines through in a different way.

Which just goes to show that energy is a personal thing. It's individualistic. "Energy is not entirely about quantity, it's also about quality," says McGee-Cooper. "And any number of things can impact it."

SMART DEFINITION

Energy level

Your capacity to meet physical, mental, and emotional challenges. Your energy level is linked to your body, mind, and spirit, and is influenced by your genetic makeup, your health, your habits and lifestyle, and your life experiences.

How the Body Creates Energy

Physically speaking, the human body creates energy out of the foods that are consumed. It converts the nutrients in foods into chemical energy (glucose) and then distributes that energy throughout the body's systems as needed.

Carbohydrates—particularly sugars and fruits—are the fuels that give you the fastest energy boost. That's because they can be quickly metabolized into glucose and promptly released into the bloodstream. Protein and fat need to be broken down more before they're useful.

That's the basic way energy is created in the body. But your energy level is also greatly influenced by factors other than what you eat.

The Enneagram and Your Personality Style

Many people look to a paradigm called the Enneagram for clues to their personalities. The Enneagram (a nine-pointed star) is a psychospiritual construct, meaning that it combines psychological and spiritual principles in an effort to help people understand themselves—and others—better.

The Enneagram divides people into nine types. Each type has "both beneficial and challenging traits," according to the International Enneagram Association (IEA):

Ones tend to be perfectionists who are diligent, conscientious, and logical. They focus their attention on getting things right and being right themselves, and can be rigid, critical, and angry.

Twos are devoted to giving to and caring for others; they are responsive and demonstrative, but can be pushy and manipulative.

Threes are performers—productive, efficient, motivated, and goal-oriented. But they can also be workaholics and obsessed with their image.

Fours are creative romantics who impose their own view on the world. They like change, because it suggests a new beginning is at hand, but they can also enjoy the role of victim and become filled with melancholy.

Fives are observant and objective and value knowledge, but can be aloof and hard to decipher.

What Dictates Your Energy Level?

Is your energy level a gift from your parents—via genetics—or is it related more to your environment and habits? "It's actually a product of both nature and nurture," says noted psychiatrist Harold H. Bloomfield, M.D., author of *The Power of 5*, among other books.

Sixes are loyal and responsible, but also skeptical, fearful, and doubting.

Sevens are fun-loving epicures who are cheerful, enthusiastic, and entertaining. But they can also be commitment-phobic and superficial.

Eights are natural leaders. They love to protect others and fight for the underdog. They easily express anger and are blunt; they can also be domineering and combative.

Nines are peacemakers who are patient and stable. They don't have much ambition, but settle for things the way they are. They are prone to tuning out the world and neglecting themselves.

Most people have a dominant Enneagram personality, with a smattering of characteristics from other types thrown into the mix. By finding your type, proponents say, you can learn more about your working and relationship styles, as well as develop ways of understanding others. (In fact, the Enneagram is now reportedly used by many businesses, government groups, therapists, and educators to enhance communication and reduce interpersonal strife.) You can gain insight into how your personality and energy level dovetail—the types of interactions and personalities that give you energy, and the types that take it away.

For more information about the Enneagram, surf to the IEA's Web site at www.intl-enneagram-assn.org.

SMART MOVE

You don't have to spend a fortune to boost your energy level. In fact, you may not have to spare a single dime. Rather than investing your time and effort looking for a magic pill or a quick fix, it's more effective to look at your lifestyle and make changes there, says Mark Meskin, Ph.D., R.D., associate professor of food, nutrition, and consumer sciences at California State Polytechnic University in Pomona, California. "The usual reasons for a lack of energy are sleep deprivation, overwork, inadequate exercise, improper nutrition, and sometimes a medical problem," he says. For a real fix, then, you need to correct these problems, instead of just applying a Band-Aid by taking a supplement, eating a candy bar, or drinking another cup of coffee.

While there is evidence that you inherit certain energy characteristics from your parents—and researchers are trying to hone in on energy genes—a high or low energy level actually stems from complex interactions between biological makeup, lifestyle habits (including how much you exercise, sleep, and eat), personality, attitude, mood, and life circumstances.

For instance, as individuals we are motivated by diverse things. "Different personality types have different drives," explains Dr. Bloomfield. "Someone who is a caregiver personality type is motivated by love, so he or she puts energy into receiving love from others. In contrast, an achiever is motivated by achievement and an adventurer is motivated by travel and new experiences." (See the Enneagram box, on pages 4 and 5 in this chapter, and chapter 2 to determine the personality and attitude traits that contribute to your energy style.)

Certainly, life events can impact energy: the death of a loved one, medical problems, mental disorders such as depression or anxiety, and high levels of stress can all sap vitality. Conversely, happy events—such as a marriage, a graduation, a new job—can give you a much needed boost.

There is also evidence that monthly and seasonal ebbs and flows can affect energy levels. Women, for example, appear to be influenced by their menstrual cycles. They may suffer from premenstrual syndrome (PMS) and feel sluggish, depressed, and irritable before menstruation due to fluctuating hormone levels or other nonhormonal factors. Many people also complain of depression and flagging energy levels during the winter months—and they may have what's known as seasonal affective disorder, or SAD. The culprit: less exposure to light during the cold season. Typically, these people feel much more energized during spring and summer, when sunlight is ample.

The Mind-Body Interaction

Energy is more than just a physical phenomenon. It also has mental, emotional, attitudinal, and spiritual components, so that for many people, a lack of energy takes the form of a loss of motivation or desire, or a dulling of one's senses and emotions, rather than just a feeling of physical tiredness. That's why it is critical to develop and maintain interests and hobbies that fascinate and excite you, and stimulate your curiosity. Without passion for something—anything—in life, mental energy is hard to come by.

The Western world has only just begun to appreciate the complex links between the mind and body in creating energy and in seeking balance. Conventional physicians have always sought hard evidence to explain bodily phenomena, and have been hard-pressed to accept scientifically inexplicable effects. Eastern cultures, on the other hand, have extensive experience in this area, rooted in two ancient methods of healing: traditional Chinese medicine and the Indian system of Ayurveda.

Chinese Medicine

Chinese medicine actually centers around the concept of energy, in the form of a powerful and vital life force, called chi (or qi, pronounced "chee").

SMART SOURCES

The Origin of Everyday Moods: Managing Energy, Tension, and Stress
Robert E. Thayer, Ph.D.

You Don't Have to Go Home from Work Exhausted!
Ann McGee-Cooper, with Duane Trammell and Barbara Lau

Boundless Energy
Deepak Chopra, M.D.

This Chi is believed to flow freely and naturally throughout the body along pathways called meridians. Both chi and the fourteen meridians through which it moves are invisible to the naked eye.

When chi is blocked, unbalanced, or weakened in the body, traditional Chinese doctors believe that illness (and a lack of energy) result. Blockages are caused by interactions between the body, mind, and spirit. Only by unblocking chi—through acupuncture or acupressure, use of herbal medicines, or other ancient techniques—can energy and wellness be restored.

Eastern medicine also emphasizes the importance of finding a balance between yin and yang. Yang is generally described as an active type of energy and is associated with day. Yin, a quiet type of energy, is associated with night. Together, though opposites, yin and yang make a whole. All of us—and for that matter, all things—have yin and yang aspects.

Ayurvedic Medicine

Ayurveda is also built around the concept of balance and energy, but in the form of the three doshas: vata, kapha, and pitta. Human beings are born with a bit of each dosha element, although we tend to take on dominant characteristics, both physically and emotionally. Most people, according to Deepak Chopra, M.D., the Indian physician and author who has done much to popularize Ayurveda in America, are "bi-doschic," meaning they have qualities of two types, rather than just a single dosha.

The **vata** dosha is symbolized by air, and is responsible for the physical functioning and the movement of the body. Vata makes the heart beat, the lungs breathe, and the blood circulate. People who are vata types tend to be very enthusiastic, excitable, and changeable, and have short bursts of mental and physical energy.

The **kapha** dosha is symbolized by earth, and governs the physical structure of the body—the muscles and tissues. Kapha types have a steady flow of energy and are relaxed and earthy.

The **pitta** dosha, which is symbolized by fire, looks over digestive and metabolic functions of the body—biochemical transformations, enzyme and hormone production. Pitta types are intense, intellectual, and driven; they also anger easily.

Each dosha type incorporates different mind-body requirements for wellness and energy. When a dosha becomes unbalanced, health problems—including fatigue—develop. To re-create balance, Ayurveda therapists prescribe a variety of remedies: yogalike movement and breathing exercises, meditation, herbs, and special diets.

Energy Ebbs and Flows

The human body's functions are subject to natural internal rhythms; medical scientists have found that our heart rates, breathing patterns, blood sugar and blood pressure levels, sleep patterns, and other biological functions fluctuate according to the time of day they're measured. So, too, each person's energy level and mood naturally vary over the course of a day.

According to Robert E. Thayer, Ph.D., professor

of biological psychology at California State University in Long Beach, California, energy tends to peak for most people in the late morning or early afternoon. It dips in the mid- to late afternoon—the notorious postlunch slump that occurs whether you eat or not—and then rises again in the early evening. It then falls as bedtime approaches.

Optimal Task Timing

In her book *Bodyrhythms: Chronobiology and Peak Performance,* science writer Lynne Lamberg offers this assessment of the optimal times to perform various tasks:

7 A.M.–8 A.M.: Arise and immediately seek some bright sun or other light to help you wake up.

9 A.M.–12 noon: Schedule the most mentally challenging tasks for morning, because alertness is high. Eleven A.M. is the best time for meetings.

1 P.M.– 2 P.M.: You're apt to be cheerful at midday, so socialize and eat lunch.

2 P.M.–3 P.M.: You're a bit sleepy now, whether or not you've had lunch. Try not to schedule meetings, tasks that require concentration, or driving for this time of the afternoon.

3 P.M.: Your postlunch slump continues, but begins to lift. It's a great time to perform mundane duties, such as filing or sorting mail.

4 P.M.: You perk up. Work on small projects—especially those that require concentration since your ability to detect errors peaks around now—and plan for the next day.

5 P.M.: Coordination, strength, and reaction time are at high levels, so schedule an exercise session.

5 P.M.–7 P.M.: Dinnertime, and your senses of smell and taste are at a high.

8 P.M.–10 P.M.: You're still alert enough to socialize, read, or pay bills.

Midnight: Go to bed, so you get seven to eight hours of sleep.

Lamberg notes that the natural body clock can be overridden, at least to a certain extent. For instance, socializing, exercise, stress, caffeine, and sugar can all give you a lift after lunch so you don't hit the slump.

Calm Energy versus Tense Energy

Psychologist Robert Thayer has created an innovative theory of energy. He believes that moods (which he defines as background feelings that persist over time) are intimately linked to energy and tension levels—and that both the mind and body are involved in producing them. Both good and bad moods have obvious impacts on energy levels, and energy levels have obvious impacts on moods.

In his book *The Origin of Everyday Moods,* Dr. Thayer describes four basic mood/energy states:

F.Y.I.

Our sleep-wake cycle is governed by a twenty-four- to twenty-five-hour internal timekeeper called the circadian rhythm. This clock resides in the brain, and causes most people to experience sleepiness during the night (between 2 A.M. and 6 A.M.), and around mid-afternoon (2 P.M.–3 P.M.) each day. Working against this biological clock can cause daytime drowsiness and a lack of energy.

• **Calm energy.** This is the optimal mood state in which you have a high level of energy, but a low tension level. You feel alert and vigorous, but also peaceful and in control. Most people rarely experience this type of energy. It's also called flow or peak performance.

• **Tense energy.** This is a more common state of being for most people. You may feel energetic, but your tension level is high, your body is tight, you're stressed, there's a sense of urgency in the air, and your energy reserves are low—but you keep going because your body is producing stress hormones (such as adrenaline) that keep you alert. You may feel a sense of power and excitement as you careen from deadline to deadline, impatiently pushing yourself from one goal to the next without taking time to refuel. Although some people describe this as a good mood, if this state persists, you're likely heading toward burnout.

• **Calm tired.** This is a state in which you're mentally and physically calm, but tired (as might occur in the late evening). It is less ideal than calm energy, but Dr. Thayer still categorizes it as a good mood.

• **Tense tired.** This is the worst mood/energy state of all. Not only are you feeling anxious and tense, but you're tired to boot. If you frequently find yourself in this mood, you may be suffering from depression, and should seek out help from a qualified professional.

Dr. Thayer says that many people don't understand the benefits of calm energy. (It's a particularly foreign concept to Westerners; other cultures are more familiar with the idea.) They believe that a high energy level can't be achieved without the presence of a slightly tense edge. "People who regularly exercise or meditate, however, understand the difference," he writes in his book. "They know what calm energy feels like, and though they have energy, they don't feel a bit tense."

Energy as You Age

As a child, you were given the gift of abundant energy. As you grow older, your physical energy level will likely decline, but your intellectual and mental energies have the capacity to remain intact and can even expand. You can develop what Ann McGee-Cooper calls "the energy of wisdom."

With every advancing year, the quality of your energy is directly related to the quality of your life, explains McGee-Cooper. Your health plays a part, of course, but your habits and the challenges you create for yourself can make the critical difference between being a peppy mature adult versus a pooped senior citizen. "Just look at people like Pablo Picasso, Thomas Edison, and Georgia O'Keeffe, to name a few, all of whom were highly productive and energetic well into their eighties. These people had an enthusiasm for their work and their lives, and were curious and passionate about learning new things. They had purpose and direction—and that made all the difference."

WHAT MATTERS, WHAT DOESN'T

What Matters
• Achieving calm energy.

• The interaction of your body, mind, and spirit.

• Your life experiences.

• Cultivating interests and challenges for yourself.

What Doesn't
• Achieving tense energy.

• Your age.

• Your sex.

Key Components of Energy Boosting

Strategies for boosting your energy level will be discussed in detail in the chapters to come, but here's a sneak preview of some of the lifestyle tips you'll learn about:

• **Get enough sleep.** Most of us need an average of seven to eight hours a night.

• **Exercise regularly.** The government recommends that all adults engage in exercise of moderate intensity five or more days a week.

• **Eat a well-balanced, healthy diet.** Follow the Food Guide Pyramid for optimal health.

• **Relieve stress.** Take steps to reduce the stress of everyday life through some exercise and relaxation techniques.

• **Find hobbies and activities that bring you joy and a sense of childlike abandon.**

• **Identify and correct mental and medical problems that can sap energy.**

Before you embark on a program to boost your pep, you first need to identify your personal energy style—which is the focus of chapter 2.

Assess Your Energy

THE KEYS

• Gain insight into your individual body rhythms.

• Assess your personal energy style.

• Learn what to include in an energy diary.

• Determine if you're more of an optimist or a pessimist.

• Uncover your brain dominance profile.

• Find out if you're a lark or a night owl—or neither.

The production and maintenance of energy is a complicated endeavor—and a very personal one, too. In your quest to optimize your energy level, you will therefore need to undertake a bit of self-assessment and to observe your habits. Then you'll probably need to make some significant changes in your lifestyle. More energy won't come without effort. But when it does, it will have been worth it.

Observe Yourself

The first step in boosting your energy level is to determine your own personal rhythms (your daily energy peaks and valleys). These natural, individual patterns—as well as certain personality traits—impact energy and make you more vulnerable to tension at certain times of the day.

How do you go about discovering your personal rhythms? All it takes is a period of self-observation during which time you take regular readings of your energy level, feelings and moods, activities and habits, and record them in a diary, such as the one on page 17.

Your Energy Diary

Buy a notebook and record your daily energy highs and lows for a week, or ideally, a full month. Several times a day—even hourly, if possible—take a moment to rate your current energy level on a scale of (1) very low, (2) low, (3) medium, or (4) high. Also write down what you are doing at the

My Daily Energy Diary

Date: Monday, April 23   Hours I slept last night   11:30 P.M.–6:30 A.M.
How well?   Fell right to sleep, woke once

Time	Energy Rating	Food or Drink	Activity Performed	Mood/Emotion
7 A.M.	2	Coffee w/s&c	Got up	Sleepy/grumpy
8 A.M.	3	Coffee w/s&c	Drove to work	More alert
9 A.M.	3			
10 A.M.	4	Muffin, coffee w/s&c	At work	Motivated
11 A.M.	4			
12 P.M.	3	Greek salad, diet soda, roll	Had lunch at desk with Sue	Happy
1 P.M.	2			
2 P.M.	1	Candy bar	Meeting	Tired/bored
3 P.M.	1	Diet soda		
4 P.M.	2			Dragging
5 P.M.	2		Went to gym for aerobics class	Hungry, didn't want to work out
6 P.M.	3	Energy bar	Still at gym	Feel so much better, glad I went
7 P.M.	3	Broiled chicken breast, rice, broccoli	Dinner	Good, alert
8 P.M.	3		On phone	Good
9 P.M.	3		Watched TV	Okay
10 P.M.	2	Potato chips, diet soda	Watched TV	Getting tired
11 P.M.	2		To bed	Tired

Overall analysis: Only experienced high energy mid-morning—can do better. First step: a better diet.

Scale: 1 = Very low; 2 = Low; 3 = Medium; 4 = High   s&c = sugar and cream

"I'm an optimist to a fault," says Connie, thirty-five, a vice president for a global bank, "and it gives me energy, mostly because it makes me try harder. I always believe I can deal with things and I always think things are going to work out. I never give up on a project."

Connie has found that it takes more energy to frown than to smile. "I know some people who are full-blown pessimists and it's a self-fulfilling prophecy: they think they can't do something, so they don't even try. It's actually very sad. Life is so much happier and more fulfilling when you look on the bright side."

time, and how you feel emotionally. Finally, record what you eat and drink (especially caffeine, sugar, and alcohol), when and how much you sleep, and what kind of physical activity you engage in, so you can look for patterns and associations. Women should also note how their menstrual cycle intersects with their energy level.

Why all the paperwork? By isolating your highs and lows you can find ways to work around them. "From your diary, you might find, for instance, that you're experiencing an energy drain because you're relying too much on coffee or sugary snacks to pick you up," says energy expert and business consultant Ann McGee-Cooper. "Correcting that situation [with better sleep, exercise, and nutrition] can boost your energy level."

Self-Assessment of Optimism/Pessimism

Psychological research reveals that optimists (positive thinkers) and pessimists (negative thinkers) have different energy predispositions. Take the self-assessment quiz on page 19, developed by psychologists Michael F. Scheier, Charles S. Carver, and Michael W. Bridges, to identify your outlook on life. Then read about how optimists and pessimists differ.

Self-Assessment Quiz 1

Answer the questions on a scale of 0 to 4:

0 = Strongly disagree
1 = Disagree
2 = Neutral
3 = Agree
4 = Strongly agree

1. In uncertain times I usually expect the best....... _____

2. It's easy for me to relax. ... _____

3. If something can go wrong for me, it will........ _____

4. I'm always optimistic about my future........... _____

5. I enjoy my friends a lot. .. _____

6. It's important for me to keep busy................ _____

7. I hardly ever expect things to go my way........ _____

8. I don't get upset too easily. .. _____

9. I rarely count on good things happening to me. ... _____

10. Overall, I expect more good things to happen to me than bad............. _____

How to Score the Test

• Add up your points for questions 1, 4, and 10: .... _____

• On questions 3, 7, and 9, give yourself:

• 0 for a 4 answer

• 1 for a 3 answer

• 2 for a 2 answer

• 3 for a 1 answer

• 4 for a 0 answer .... _____

• Disregard your answers to questions 2, 5, 6, and 8. (These questions are merely fillers.)

• Now total your score: ..... _____

What Your Score Means

19 to 24: You're a full-tilt optimist.

15 to 18: You've got strong optimistic tendencies.

10 to 14: You're neutral—neither a real optimist nor a real pessimist. In fact, depending on the situation, you might exhibit either tendency.

5 to 9: You've got strong pessimistic tendencies.

0 to 4: You're a full-tilt pessimist.

From M. F. Scheier, C. S. Carver, and M. W. Bridges, "Revised Life Orientation Test (LOT-R)," *Journal of Personality and Social Psychology,* vol. 67, 1994, p. 1073. Copyright American Psychological Association; reprinted with permission.

SMART SOURCES

*Bodyrhythms: Chrono-
   biology and Peak
   Performance*
Lynne Lamberg

Learned Optimism
Martin E. P. Seligman,
   Ph.D.

What's the Difference?

What's the difference between optimists and pessimists in terms of energy? Optimists—those who
perceive the glass as half full—exude energy. They
see positive signs of what they're looking and hoping for all around them, and recognize them as
such. They make their own luck and take whatever life hands them and try to turn it to their
advantage. Their positive, hopeful attitude helps
them to persist at a task or goal until they succeed.
Optimists try harder and are energized by challenges. As a result, they tend to be more successful
at school, work, and sports, and even have better
health and perhaps longer lifespans than pessimists, reports Martin E. P. Seligman, Ph.D., presi-
dent-elect of the American Psychological Association
and author of *Learned Optimism.*

Pessimists—those who often see the glass as
half empty—exude exhaustion. They find negative signs all around them, and register them as
proof positive that nothing turns out the way they
would want it to. Each perceived negative sign is
simply another nail in the coffin, and prompts
them to give up. Pessimists are also more prone to
depression than optimists.

It appears that about a quarter of the propensity to take a bright versus dim view of life is inborn;
the rest comes from your life experiences and circumstances. "You may learn some negative beliefs
or attitudes from your family—but you can unlearn
them, too," says McGee-Cooper. "You don't have to
perpetuate pessimistic thinking." (See chapter 6
for techniques to overcome a propensity to pessimism.)

Self-Assessment of Brain Dominance

Like your attitude, your brain-dominance profile—whether you are primarily left-brained or right-brained in your approach to tasks—plays a key role in determining your energy level.

"Most of us have a dominant brain hemisphere, just as most of us have a dominant hand," explains McGee-Cooper. "Although we can use both sides of the brain, we favor one side over the other in terms of the way we think and act. In other words, when we have a choice, we use that preferred side, just as we use our preferred hand to write." Thus, by identifying your natural brain-dominance profile and developing a style of living and working that complements it, you can quickly and effectively boost your energy level.

Before we get into the qualities of the left- versus the right-brained person, however, take the self-assessment quiz on pages 22 to 25 (developed by McGee-Cooper for use in business settings) to obtain your personal profile.

F.Y.I.

Energy expert Ann McGee-Cooper says that introverts—those who naturally turn inward—gain energy by spending time alone, whereas extroverts—those who naturally turn outward—build pep by socializing with others.

Professor Robert E. Thayer, Ph.D., of California State University, in Long Beach, adds that introverts tend to experience energy highs early in the day, whereas extroverts peak later.

Self-Assessment Quiz 2

Read through the following list of statements and quickly decide which tasks give you energy and which drain your energy. Circle the number that best represents your energy response to the task. The scale ranges from "5" (for a task or behavior that highly energizes you) to "–5" (for a task that leaves you energy-depleted).

If you find that on some statements you have both responses (sometimes you get energy from this situation and sometimes it drains your energy), then score twice on that line—once for the degree of energy gain and once for the degree of energy drain.

1. I enjoy and get energy from creating options such as making "to-do" lists, brainstorming many possible places to go on vacation, thinking of lots of possible ways to do a project. In meetings, I can get interested in a new idea and get energy by adding lots of ideas to it.

Energy Gain						Energy Drain				
5	4	3	2	1	0	–1	–2	–3	–4	–5
					(neutral)					

2. I get energy from creating order and organizing. I enjoy going through piles of stuff and eliminating the unnecessary. In meetings, I get energy by bringing agenda items to closure and knowing specific tasks are assigned and will be followed up.

Energy Gain						Energy Drain				
5	4	3	2	1	0	–1	–2	–3	–4	–5
					(neutral)					

3. I get my creative juices going by having lots of materials out to work with. Typically I have lots of stuff around me in my work area.

Energy Gain						Energy Drain				
5	4	3	2	1	0	–1	–2	–3	–4	–5
					(neutral)					

4. I typically leave my desk and work area straight and clean, primarily because I get energy from putting things back in their places and like to work in a clean, neat area. This seems to apply equally to projects at home, such as yard work.

Energy Gain						Energy Drain				
5	4	3	2	1	0	–1	–2	–3	–4	–5
					(neutral)					

5. I enjoy and get energized by juggling several tasks at once and by moving from one to the other intuitively. As I tire of one job or get blocked on how to proceed, I shift and work awhile on another task. This is energizing for me and I often get ideas for one project by putting it out of my mind and working on something completely different.

Energy Gain   Energy Drain
5   4   3   2   1   0   −1 −2 −3 −4 −5
                (neutral)

6. I get energy by finishing one thing before I move on to the next. I prefer to create and follow an orderly process in my work. I accomplish the high-priority tasks first and then move on to lower priorities.

Energy Gain   Energy Drain
5   4   3   2   1   0   −1 −2 −3 −4 −5
                (neutral)

7. I seem to get energy from being unpredictable. I like to keep all my options open and find being flexible and spontaneous easy and energizing.

Energy Gain   Energy Drain
5   4   3   2   1   0   −1 −2 −3 −4 −5
                (neutral)

8. I get energy from being predictable and want others to do the same for me. I enjoy planning and keeping on schedule. I like to plan ahead and know well in advance what is coming.

Energy Gain   Energy Drain
5   4   3   2   1   0   −1 −2 −3 −4 −5
                (neutral)

9. I get energy from breaking old rules and policies and finding new ways to get things done. I frequently find rules and policies limiting.

Energy Gain   Energy Drain
5   4   3   2   1   0   −1 −2 −3 −4 −5
                (neutral)

10. I prefer to follow the rules and wish others would as well. For me, policies and structure help things to run consistently and smoothly. I get energy by providing a positive role model for "going by the book."

Energy Gain   Energy Drain
5   4   3   2   1   0   −1 −2 −3 −4 −5
                (neutral)

11. I get energy by risking. I seem to leave things until the last minute and frequently race to meet an important deadline or have to rush in traffic to get places on time. Racing in at the eleventh hour seems to give me a rush of adrenaline. I perform well under pressure.

Energy Gain   Energy Drain
5   4   3   2   1   0   −1 −2 −3 −4 −5
                (neutral)

12. I get energy by planning ahead in detail and allowing a safety "cushion" of time so that I won't lose energy by

(continued on page 24)

getting pressured into a mad rush at the last minute. I pride myself on being prompt and am usually early to most appointments and meetings.

Energy Gain   Energy Drain
5 4 3 2 1 0 −1 −2 −3 −4 −5
(neutral)

13. I get energy by "flying by the seat of my pants" on projects and other assignments. When specifications are too detailed, there is not as much opportunity for me to get into it and innovate. I prefer a wide-open assignment and enjoy the challenge of a spur-of-the-moment need to respond without lots of planning or rehearsal.

Energy Gain   Energy Drain
5 4 3 2 1 0 −1 −2 −3 −4 −5
(neutral)

14. I prefer to plan and rehearse. I want to have a clear idea of what I am going to do and what is expected of me well before the deadline. "Flying by the seat of my pants" is not my best style. I get energy by having the time to coordinate my plans with others.

Energy Gain   Energy Drain
5 4 3 2 1 0 −1 −2 −3 −4 −5
(neutral)

15. I get energy by tackling the impossible. The bigger the challenge, the more I like it. In fact, when things get too easy I may even subconsciously cause a little crisis just to keep things stirred up.

Energy Gain   Energy Drain
5 4 3 2 1 0 −1 −2 −3 −4 −5
(neutral)

16. I get energy by implementing solutions. Once a new project has been conceptualized, my strong suit is to manage the project to completion.

Energy Gain   Energy Drain
5 4 3 2 1 0 −1 −2 −3 −4 −5
(neutral)

17. I do my research, but I trust my intuition and get energy by leaving things a bit open. I like to go into a situation without too much preconditioning so my intuition can work. For example, in a sales call or project negotiation, I trust my ability to listen to and read the client and respond in the moment, so I don't do a lot of rehearsal and tight planning prior to the event.

Energy Gain   Energy Drain
5 4 3 2 1 0 −1 −2 −3 −4 −5
(neutral)

18. I get energy by rehearsing all the options before starting. I probably put more time than most into planning and research, but this is my strong suit and I enjoy this part of the job.

Energy Gain   Energy Drain
5   4   3   2   1   0   −1 −2 −3 −4 −5
            (neutral)

19. I get energy with a new challenge. I find myself more challenged if I move on to a new job or position every three years or so. For me the big energy comes at the beginning when I am trying to get on top of the assignment and see the big picture. Once I have the job in hand, I begin to lose energy and interest. Then I find myself looking for a new challenge.

Energy Gain   Energy Drain
5   4   3   2   1   0   −1 −2 −3 −4 −5
            (neutral)

20. I get energy when I've been at a job for long enough to reach mastery. I like to stay with a job five to seven years at least. I feel that I do my best work in a new assignment after I've learned all the ropes.

Energy Gain   Energy Drain
5   4   3   2   1   0   −1 −2 −3 −4 −5
            (neutral)

How to Score the Test

Now go back and total your scores on the odd-numbered questions (1, 3, 5, 7, 9, etc.) for energy gains ___ and energy drains___. These questions describe more right-brained processes, so if you have a high energy gain score here (and a low energy drain score), most likely you are a dominant right-brained person.

Next, total your scores on the even-numbered questions (2, 4, 6, 8, etc.) for energy gains___ and energy drains____. These describe a classic left-brained preference. If you have high energy gain scores for these questions and low energy drains, very likely your mental processing is dominant left-brain.

And what if your scores seem balanced with energy gains from both odd- and even-numbered answers? If your energy gain scores are high on the majority, you probably have already discovered your own ways of using your two hemispheres as supportive partners. We call this profile *brain integration.* However, if you use both systems represented by the twenty questions but still end most days feeling drained or wiped out, then you may be using both hemispheres but one against the other—a process called *duality.*

Children are typically larks. They wake up early and go to bed early. Yet once puberty hits, children become owls—in fact, teens are notorious for staying up late and sleeping in. The interesting news: A recent Brown University study suggests that this adolescent phenomenon isn't just rebellion, it's biological.

Research also suggests that teens need about nine hours of sleep (versus the adult's average eight) and that many adolescents are suffering from chronic sleep deficits induced by early-morning classes—which lead them to sleep even longer on weekends in an effort to catch up.

What's the Difference?

Left-brained people think in a logical, rational, linear, fact-based manner. They follow rules and conform, are analytical, all business, and all adult.

Right-brained people think in an illogical, fanciful way. They're creative, intuitive, playful, spontaneous, and flexible; like children in many ways.

"I've learned that dominant right-brained people will experience an energy surge if they engage in certain activities, such as experimenting with many different solutions to a problem," explains McGee-Cooper. "If dominant left-brained people perform the same tasks, however, they'll experience an energy drain." (Left-brained people feel more comfortable and energized following a set, predictable, and methodical procedure.)

Attemping to work against your natural brain-dominance will sap energy and create tension.

The ultimate goal is to integrate both right- and left-brain tendencies so that—not to be facetious—you become a "whole-brained" rather than "half-brained" person. Using your whole brain builds energy; using only your favored half or pitting one side of the brain against the other creates imbalance and depletes energy. In the work environment, for instance, if you're strictly using the left side of your brain, you may be so rigid, structured, and inflexible that you can't cope with fast change. That means you'll be out of step with your coworkers, McGee-Cooper notes. On the other hand, if you only use the right side, you'll be so scattered that you won't be able to focus on or finish anything. Either way, you'll probably feel overworked and exhausted.

Integrating the two brain hemispheres is particularly of importance because McGee-Cooper has recently found that "hemisphericity" actually changes during the course of the day. "We have a need to shift hemispheres and use the other side of the brain. What you find energizing in the morning may be de-energizing later, and ignoring the need to shift hemispheres could cause an energy slump. For instance, I'm more right-brained in the morning. I am ready to tackle a hundred projects all at once. I love to juggle and jump from one project to the next depending on my mood and inspiration—and without necessarily finishing each task first. And I'm more left-brained in the afternoon. I feel scattered and frustrated if I take the shotgun approach; that's when I need more organization and closure to maintain my energy."

Self-Assessment of Lark/Owl Tendencies

Although most people are "standard circadian types," (awakening around 7 A.M., peaking in mid-morning, slumping after lunch, and perking up again in late afternoon and early evening, and then getting sleepy and retiring around 11 P.M. or midnight), a small group of individuals displays distinct day-night preferences.

"Larks"—about 10 percent of the population—tend to be most energetic soon after awakening and peak two hours earlier than standard circadian types. "Owls"—also about 10 percent of the population—experience their greatest bursts of energy later in the day.

To evaluate whether you have lark/owl tendencies, take the following quiz.

SMART DEFINITION

Lark and Owl

A lark is a morning person—someone whose energy level is highest in the morning and midday. An owl—a night person— is someone whose energy level doesn't reach its highest point until later in the day and evening.

Self-Assessment Quiz 3

For each question, check the answer that best describes your living habits, and then circle the point score on the same line:

Questions	Points
1. What time would you get up if you were entirely free to plan your day?	
• Before 7 A.M.	1
• 7 A.M.–9 A.M.	2
• After 9 A.M.	3
2. How easy is it for you to get up on workdays?	
• Very difficult	3
• Moderately difficult/ depends on the day	2
• Fairly easy	1
3. How alert do you feel during the first thirty minutes after you get up in the morning?	
• Alert/fresh	1
• Varies	2
• Sleepy/tired	3

Questions	Points
4. What time would you go to bed if it were completely up to you?	
• After midnight	3
• 10:30 P.M.–midnight	2
• Before 10:30 P.M.	1
5. How sleepy/tired are you one and a half hours before going to bed during the work week?	
• Very tired/ready to fall asleep	1
• Moderately tired/depends on the day	2
• Not very tired	3

Questions	Points

6. When you've stayed up later than usual, assuming you didn't have any alcohol, when do you wake up the next morning?

- Later than usual, with a desire to fall back asleep — 3
- Varies — 2
- At your usual time, with a desire to get out of bed — 1

How to Score the Test
Add up the number of points.

What Your Score Means
If you scored 6 to 7 points, you're an extreme lark; if you scored 8 to 9 points, you are considered a moderate lark. Extreme larks like to get out of bed as early as 4 A.M. or 5 A.M. and to go to bed by 9 P.M. or 10 P.M. Their periods of high alertness occur about two hours earlier than do those of people with standard circadian profiles, and they do their best work of the day around 8 A.M. or 9 A.M.

If you scored 10 to 14 points, you are neither a lark nor an owl. Actually, you have no particular tendency; like most people, you have a standard circadian profile. The standard profile finds a person feeling comfortable waking up between 7 A.M. and 8 A.M. and usually going to bed between 11 P.M. and midnight. In between, most people have periods of high alertness in the morning and early evening and often experience a period of low alertness in the early afternoon.

If you scored 15 to 16 points, you are a moderate owl; if you scored 17 to 18, you are an extreme owl. True owls like to sleep into the late morning, and usually have no trouble staying awake and alert past 2 A.M. or 3 A.M. Their periods of high alertness and sleepiness occur about two hours later than those of people who have standard circadian profiles.

WHAT MATTERS, WHAT DOESN'T

What Matters
• Your individual daily body rhythms.

• Your optimism profile.

• Your dominant brain hemisphere.

• Your lark/owl tendencies.

What Doesn't
• Your family's negative attitudes.

• The hand you've been dealt (you can make your own luck).

• A natural propensity for pessimism.

If you're considering taking a job that requires you to work the night shift, your lark/owl profile can help you predict how well you'll adapt to the "off" hours. According to Circadian Technologies, a research and consulting firm in Cambridge, Massachusetts, that investigates the implications of circadian rhythms, owls find it easier to adjust to night work because their times of alertness start later and are aligned with being awake at night.

Adding It All Up

Okay, now you're ready to draw some conclusions.

First, review your diary data and try to isolate your peak energy periods and energy slumps during the day. If you're mathematically inclined, try to plot out your highs and lows on graph paper.

Second, assess the results of the three quizzes. For instance, if you're an optimist, you already have the battle half licked, and you can turn to other areas of your life to enhance energy. But if the quiz shows you're neutral or a pessimist, you'll want to find ways to adopt a more positive attitude (see chapter 6). Likewise, if you discover you have distinct day or night energy preferences, you'll want to try working your schedule around these tendencies. And if you're only using one side of your brain—or the two sides are dueling—you'll need to develop techniques for achieving integration. Again, see chapter 6 for suggestions.

Third, take a look at the box on page 31 and check off some things you've learned from keeping your diary and taking the quizzes; add in any guesses you have about behaviors that may be affecting your energy.

My Energy Profile

From My Diary (gauge your response for each)

Daily high energy times:

Daily low energy times:

Weekly high energy times:

Weekly low energy times:

Monthly high energy times:

Monthly low energy times:

From the Quizzes (circle one option in each group)

I am: an optimist   a pessimist

I am: left-brained   right-brained

I am: integrated   dueling

I have a: standard circadian profile
moderate lark profile
extreme lark profile
moderate owl profile
extreme owl profile

Behaviors That Could Be Affecting My Energy Level (circle all that apply)

• Sleep (not enough, too much, not deeply enough, too much napping)

• Drinking too much coffee and other caffeinated beverages

• Drinking too much alcohol

• Eating too much sugar

• Skipping meals

• Not eating a well-balanced diet

• Not eating enough calories

• Being overweight

• Not exercising enough

• Stress

• Depression

• Medical problems

• Depression or anxiety

• PMS

• Not having enough time for myself

• Not taking breaks for vacations from work or the kids

• Not having a sense of purpose in life

• Not having a hobby, craft, or sport to pursue in my leisure time

Keep this energy profile on hand to refer to as you read the chapters to come. You'll want to use your self-assessment data to isolate where you're already doing things to enhance your energy, where your behaviors are depleting it, and where you can make improvements.

So, what's next on the agenda? In chapter 3, we'll review some of the primary medical and psychological causes of fatigue and a lack of energy.

THE BOTTOM LINE

Several personality and physiologic characteristics can impact your energy level, including your tendency to optimism or pessimism, your brain-dominance profile, and whether you function significantly better in the morning or at night.

Keeping an observation diary is the best way to clue in to your energy peaks and dips, and the behaviors that may be preventing you from achieving a more constant, high flow of energy.

CHAPTER 3

....

Energy Zappers

Because energy is a product of both body and mind, any number of physical and psychological ailments can undermine your efforts to boost your zip—largely by producing fatigue.

"Fatigue is so common that half of patients who visit a family physician complain of it," says Richard N. Podell, M.D., an integrative physician practicing in New Providence, New Jersey, and author of *Patient Power: How to Protect Yourself from Medical Error*. Oftentimes, it's merely a symptom of modern-day life (a poor diet, too little sleep, not enough exercise). But fatigue can also be due to an identifiable and treatable medical illness.

Here, then, are some of the top psychological and medical problems that zap you of needed energy.

Stress

Stress is ubiquitous in modern life. Actually, you couldn't live without it, since it provides you with the physical capacity—through the release of stress hormones—to react to your environment and its demands, and to resist threats to your health and well-being. Whether its fighting or fleeing a dangerous situation or combatting an infection, the stress response is key to your continued survival.

Stress motivates you (when it's of a manageable size), but it can also easily overwhelm you. It's all in the way you perceive stress—which is a very individual phenomenon. Some people find huge amounts of stress exhilarating—breakneck deadlines are their spice of life. Others find that kind of pressure toxic. Some can handle stress well for short periods of time, but break down when it continues for long stretches.

There's also another component to the stress equation: how well you adapt to stress. Many people overreact to mildly stressful situations—annoying phone calls, traffic, tight deadlines—and their minds and bodies shift to an always-alert mode; in other words, they're chronically stressed. Others have learned to calm themselves so that minor stresses don't overtax them. (Ironically, psychologists say that it's the small, daily stresses that are most deleterious to health and energy, as opposed to the large, infrequent stresses, such as a catastrophic accident or death in the family.)

Unabating stress—real or perceived, large or small—takes a tremendous toll on physical and mental health, weakens the immune system, and is linked to two of the top causes of death, cancer and heart disease. No surprise, here, but it's also associated with a distinct lack of pep.

Symptoms

- Fatigue

- Anger or irritability

- Anxiety

- Depression

- Tension headaches

- Dizziness

- Sweaty palms

SMART DEFINITION

Stress hormones

Cortisol and adrenaline are two hormones that are made by the body in response to stress. In small amounts, they rally the body's resources to increase the chances of survival. In excess, they actually decrease the chances of survival (at least over the long term).

Too much cortisol and adrenaline can have many damaging effects on the body: they raise cholesterol levels, weaken the heart, harden the arteries, depress the immune system, and damage brain cells.

- Shortness of breath

- Chest pain

- Back pain

- Jaw pain (also known as temporomandibular joint disorder or TMD)

- Body aches and pains

- Stomach upset

- Diarrhea

- Constipation

- Heartburn

- Irritable bowel syndrome

- Ulcer

- Heart palpitations

- Frequent colds and flus

- Sleep disturbances

Treatment

Once identified—which can be difficult to do since many of the symptoms mimic medical diseases—stress can be resolved via a number of routes. Learning and regularly performing relaxation techniques such as meditation, deep breathing, yoga, and visualization are critical to stopping the stress response. Exercise is another key. So is eating well. In fact, almost all of the suggestions found in this book can not only increase your energy level—they can also reduce stress.

Anxiety Disorders

Anxiety is the most common mental health problem known to Americans—about 65 million people suffer from it annually—and it affects twice as many women as men. Over the course of a lifetime, one out of every two people will experience some form of mild to moderate anxiety lasting for two weeks or longer.

Anxiety is intricately linked to our response to stress. According to psychiatrist Harold H. Bloomfield, M.D., who recently authored the book *Healing Anxiety with Herbs*, anxiety is "an overreaction in the first stage of the body's stress response, the alarm ('fight or flight') reaction." In people with anxiety, the brain's alarm center, the amygdala, signals the body and mind that there is a five-alarm fire when really there's only smoke. A tendency toward fearful, worrisome thinking patterns contributes to the problem. Anxiety sufferers also appear to have low levels of serotonin, a brain chemical that acts as a natural tranquilizer.

As with stress, a little anxiety is natural, normal, and manageable. But anxiety can also easily veer out of control, producing mild to moderate to severe symptoms. It can percolate quietly in the background or take center stage in your life—and can last weeks, months, or even years.

Symptoms

• Alarm, panic, dread, terror

• Jumpiness

• Heart palpitations

• Trembling

• Cold, sweaty hands

• Dizziness

• Muscle aches and pains

• Fast, shallow breathing (hyperventilation)

• Nausea

• Diarrhea

• Headaches

• Fatigue

• Depression

Treatment

Only a quarter of the 65 million people suffering from anxiety annually receive adequate treatment for it, reports Dr. Bloomfield. Those who do seek and receive treatment will often be prescribed tranquilizing drugs such as Valium and Xanax.

Before opting for medication, you may want to look into alternative self-help remedies, such as exercise, relaxation techniques, and herbs—kava, St. John's wort (hypericum), Siberian ginseng, and valerian, for example. These remedies are now being touted as equally effective but supposed safer ways to relieve mild-to-moderate forms of anxiety, improve sleep, bolster the nervous system, and guard against stress. (More severe cases of anxiety, however, still require drug treatment and/or psychotherapy.)

Emotional Loss and Depression

It doesn't take a brain specialist to figure out that depression can sap vitality. But did you know that suffering the blues is incredibly common? Depression affects 9 to 15 million Americans yearly, and women have double the risk of men of experiencing a severe episode. Symptoms can range from mild to severely incapacitating (what's known as major or clinical depression).

Oftentimes, depression may be prompted by a catastrophic emotional event: the death of a loved one, the loss of a job, a failure of some sort, a divorce, financial problems, an accident, and any number of other traumatic events. All of these situations can raise your stress level, provoking feelings of hopelessness and helplessness, and leading to anxiety, depression, and a loss of energy.

SMART MOVE

Herbs can often be a smart alternative to medical therapies.

St. John's wort, for instance, can cost as little as thirty cents a day or approximately $10 a month, says Harold H. Bloomfield, M.D. Compare that to the $200 to $300 a month charged for the antidepressant drug Prozac.

"Herbs can be as effective as synthetic drugs, are nonaddictive, and have far fewer, if any, of the plaguing side effects of the most popularly prescribed drugs," he reports. They're also widely available without a prescription from health food shops and drugstores.

As for other "alternative remedies": exercise is free, a better diet is yours for the asking, and relaxation techniques are there to be learned and used.

SMART SOURCES

American Psychological
   Association
800-964-2000
www.helping.apa.org

Request free brochure
*Talk to Someone Who
Can Help* or ask for a
referral.

Depression Aware-
   ness, Recognition,
   and Treatment
   (D/ART) Program
National Institute of
   Mental Health
5600 Fishers Lane,
   Room 10-85
Rockville, MD 20857
800-421-4211
www.nimh.nih.gov

Request *Let's Talk
About Depression* and
other free brochures.

Anxiety Disorders
   Education Program
National Institute of
   Mental Health
5600 Fishers Lane,
   Room 7-99
Rockville, MD 20857
888-8ANXIETY
www.nimh.nih.gov

Request *Anxiety Disor-
ders* and other free
brochures.

Symptoms

- Persistent down, anxious, or empty feelings

- Low energy, fatigue

- Loss of interest or pleasure in your usual activities

- Sleep disturbances

- Appetite and weight changes

- Feelings of hopelessness

- Feelings of guilt, worthlessness, or helplessness

- Thoughts of death or suicide

- Difficulty concentrating, remembering, or making decisions

- Persistent aches and pains for which doctors can't find a physical cause

If you experience five or more of the symptoms listed above for longer than two weeks, see a doctor for evaluation and treatment.

Treatment

Depression is now recognized as a medical disorder, largely because it has been linked to physical changes in the brain (most notably, low levels of the brain chemicals serotonin and norepinephrine). Although mild-to-moderate depression often resolves on its own, whether you seek treatment or not, more severe depression usually requires psychotherapy and/or medication.

A number of drugs have been developed to correct the chemical imbalance characteristic of depression. These include the selective serotonin reuptake inhibitors (SSRIs), including Prozac, Zoloft, and Paxil; tricyclic antidepressants (TCAs) such as Elavil and Pamelor; and some newer antidepressants such as Effexor and Remeron. Studies demonstrate that going on drug therapy *doubles* the chance that depression will improve or disappear within two to four months.

Alternative, nondrug remedies are also gaining credibility for the relief of mild-to-moderate depression:

• **Exercise.** Several psychological studies have found that regular activity sessions can improve depression as much as long- or short-term psychotherapies. Continuous, rhythmic exercises such as swimming, walking, biking, jogging, and rowing seem to have the most positive effects on altering mood, says Thomas Plante, Ph.D., associate professor of psychology at Santa Clara University in Santa Clara, California. "Don't exercise too hard, too long, or do anything competitive, however," he cautions, "as that can make you feel worse instead of better."

• **St. John's wort (hypericum).** Results from more than twenty European studies comparing standard antidepressants and placebo with this herb indicate that it is just as effective as synthetic antidepressants. (Like antidepressants, it helps 50 to 80 percent of people.) Hypericum also appears to work in much the same way as antidepressants—

by boosting serotonin levels in the brain, says Dr. Bloomfield. It may also inhibit excess production of the stress hormone cortisol.

Sleep Deprivation

Sleep deprivation is prevalent in the United States and has an obvious impact on energy. Lack of sleep reduces alertness and affects mood, coordination, memory, and physical reaction times. It also puts a damper on your performance and your enjoyment of life.

The table below shows that the average adult

How Much Sleep We Get versus How Much We Need

Although no two people need the same amount of sleep, researchers offer these approximations:

Life Stage	Sleep We Get (hours)	Sleep We Need (hours)
Infant	18	18
Child	10–12	10–12
Adolescent/ young adult	6	10
Adult	Less than 7	7–9
Older adult	5–7	8

needs seven to nine hours of sleep a night. Yet during the workweek, many Americans sleep six hours or less per night.

Even when we can sleep, sleep quality tends to be poor for many of us. According to the National Sleep Foundation (NSF):

• Forty million Americans suffer from sleep disorders (of which there are eighty identified types, including insomnia and sleep apnea [lapses of breathing during sleep]).

• Twenty to thirty million people have occasional sleep problems, usually caused by pain, stress, anxiety, depression, or illness.

• One in two people say they have trouble sleeping occasionally.

• Sixty-three million Americans report being sleepy during the day.

Symptoms

• An inability to fall asleep or to stay asleep

• Daytime drowsiness

• Excessive snoring

• Unpleasant leg sensations that awaken you (a sign of restless leg syndrome)

SMART SOURCES

National Sleep Foundation
729 Fifteenth St., NW, 4th Floor
Washington, D.C. 20005
www.sleepfoundation. org

Request brochures such as *The Nature of Sleep* and *Sleep and the Traveler.*

Treatment

Oftentimes, doctors will suggest lifestyle changes to help you overcome a sleeping disorder. These suggestions vary depending on the nature of the problem. You may be told to schedule naps into your day, take warm baths a few hours before bedtime, not spend too much time in bed when you're not sleeping, exercise in the afternoon, reduce your alcohol intake, and expose yourself to bright light during certain parts of the day. You may also be prescribed medications; the newest drugs such as Ambien are not as addictive and don't cause as much daytime sleepiness as Valium and other older medications. They are for short-term use only, however.

If you suffer from excessive snoring or sleep apnea—which means you have short periods during sleep when you stop breathing—surgery may be advised.

See chapter 6 for more details and further tips on improving sleep.

Hypothyroidism

An underfunctioning thyroid, or hypothyroidism, is a common and subtle cause of tiredness, especially in women over age forty. About 6 to 7 million Americans suffer from this problem, in which the tiny, butterfly-shaped gland that regulates body growth and metabolism ceases to produce enough thyroid hormone to keep your body humming. A test called the sensitive TSH blood test can easily home in on the problem; it can also detect what is known as subclinical or early hypothyroidism. That's important, because beginning treatment when dysfunction is mild can pre-vent progression of the disease.

Left uncorrected, hypothyroidism can impair fertility, dangerously increase cholesterol levels, and permanently damage the thyroid gland and other organs.

Symptoms

- Fatigue

- Loss of interest and/or pleasure

- Forgetfulness

- Dry, coarse hair

- Loss of eyebrow hair

- Puffy face and eyes

- Enlargement of the thyroid gland (called goiter)

- Dry skin

- Intolerance to cold

- Weight gain

- Heavy menstrual periods

- Constipation

- Brittle nails

- Slow heartbeat

STREET SMARTS

When Heidi, thirty-six, started to feel unex-pectedly sluggish, her first thought was that she was overdoing it. So she cut back and tried to rest more. She took naps but would wake up as tired as when she laid down; even a good night's sleep didn't leave her feeling restored. Over the course of six months, her fatigue worsened. Her doctor tested her for a variety of ailments—pregnancy, Lyme disease, mononu-cleosis, anemia, and fi-nally thyroid dysfunc-tion. He found that her thyroid was slightly un-deractive and producing too little of the hor-mones it was supposed to (a condition known as hypothyroidism).

Heidi's disease was caught early and she began taking thyroid re-placement pills. Since then, she's back to nor-mal. "Thyroid disease is easily treatable," she says. "I feel like my old energetic self again."

The Other Side of the Coin: Hyperthyroidism

The thyroid cannot only become sluggish, it can also get revved up and start producing too much thyroid hormone. This is called hyperthyroidism. The result: you feel overly peppy, restless, perhaps experience a rapid heartbeat, and lose weight without even trying. Other symptoms can include nervousness; irritability; sleeping difficulties; bulging eyes; an unblinking stare; enlargement of the thyroid gland (called a goiter); excessive perspiration; an intolerance to heat; infrequent menstrual periods; more frequent bowel movements; warm, moist palms; and a fine tremor in the fingers.

As with hypothyroidism, treatment of hyperthyroidism is fairly simple. The most common approach is the use of radioactive iodine to shrink and disable the gland; antithyroid drugs may also be prescribed.

Treatment

A daily thyroid hormone replacement pill for life can correct hypothyroidism. Since your requirements change over time, however, you'll also need to get regular sensitive TSH tests to ensure that you're receiving the proper dosage.

Chronic Fatigue Syndrome

Chronic fatigue syndrome (CFS) is a prolonged, debilitating illness characterized by severe fatigue and multiple, vague symptoms. Approximately four to ten new cases occur per 100,000 American adults yearly, most of them in women between the ages of thirty and fifty.

CFS is tough to diagnose, and until recently wasn't accepted as a legitimate illness. A cause for the syndrome has not yet been discovered—some believe it's set off by a virus—but it's suspected there are any number of triggers for it.

Symptoms

• Severe to incapacitating fatigue that worsens with physical activity

• Headaches

• Recurrent sore throats

• Tender lymph nodes

• Muscle and joint pains

• Insomnia

• Inability to concentrate

• Forgetfulness

• Anxiety

• Depression

SMART SOURCES

The Chronic Fatigue and Immune Dysfunction Syndrome (CFIDS) Association 800-442-3437

Advocacy and support group for people with chronic fatigue syndrome; request a free general information packet.

Centers for Disease Control and Prevention www.cdc.gov

Surf to section on chronic fatigue syndrome.

Treatment

The best advice doctors currently can offer people with CFS is to rest as often as possible and to reduce stress. There's some evidence that mild exercise can be helpful, as may visits to a counselor if you are depressed or anxious.

Drug therapy is limited. Doctors may suggest analgesics to counter headaches and other aches and pains. And they may prescribe antidepressants to lift depression, aid sleep, and decrease pain.

Iron-Deficiency Anemia

A lack of iron in the blood is the most common form of nutritional deficiency in the United States, particularly among women. Researchers recently estimated that a whopping 7.8 million adolescent girls and women of childbearing age suffer from iron deficiency, and approximately 3.3 million of these women have anemia (iron-poor blood) as a result. The disorder is typically caused by a diet lacking in iron or, more commonly, by chronic bleeding (perhaps from a bleeding ulcer or polyp or excessive menstrual blood loss).

The government recommends screenings for all nonpregnant women every five to ten years for anemia; women at high risk for anemia—those who experience heavy menstrual periods, low iron intake, or a previous diagnosis of iron-deficiency anemia—should have tests annually.

Symptoms

- Fatigue

- Pale skin

- Weakness

- Faintness

- Breathlessness

- Heart palpitations

Treatment

Iron-deficiency anemia isn't usually life threatening, but it does significantly impact your quality of life (and your energy level).

If excessive bleeding is the cause of the problem, correcting it will usually resolve anemia as well. If a poor diet is to blame, increasing your intake of iron-rich foods (meats and other proteins) and foods that increase iron absorption (such as citrus fruits and other sources containing vitamin C) will help. Iron supplements are only recommended when a doctor monitors your use of them.

Diabetes

Some 16 million Americans have diabetes mellitus—and half don't know it, reports the American

SMART SOURCES

Healthfinder
www.healthfinder.gov

This government-sponsored Web site is a gateway to credible health sites, databases, and self-help groups.

Ask Dr. Weil
cgi.pathfinder.com/
    drweil

The popular alternative medicine guru, Andrew Weil, M.D., will answer medical questions posed by visitors to this Web site.

Diabetes Association. About eighteen hundred new cases of the disease are diagnosed each day.

There are two types of diabetes:

• **Type 1,** or insulin-dependent diabetes, typically starts in childhood and is characterized by little or no insulin production by the pancreas. This makes it impossible for the body to effectively metabolize carbohydrates when they are eaten. (Carbohydrates are broken down into glucose, which is sent into the blood, where it is ferried by insulin into various cells, and then burned to make energy for the muscles. When no insulin is available to take glucose out of the blood, a dangerous overload can occur.)

• **Type 2,** adult-onset diabetes, the far more common type, usually starts after age forty. The pan-

Insulin Resistance

Insulin resistance is a condition in which the body does not respond appropriately to the release of insulin. It is estimated that 25 percent of adults suffer from insulin resistance, and it is often a precursor to diabetes and heart disease.

Some nutrition experts believe that insulin resistance is the result of eating too many carbohydrates. They say that when you consume a lot carbohydrates, they are digested quickly and spur the body to produce insulin in excess. The body eventually becomes numb—resistant—to the excessive insulin, which causes it to churn out even more. This, in turn, creates cravings for more carbohydrates, which makes you eat more and gain weight.

The carb-makes-you-fat theory is a controversial one (and the reasoning behind many fad protein diets today like *The Zone* and *Protein Power*). No one disputes that insulin resistance is a real problem, especially for many diabetics, but whether carbohydrates are to blame is questionable. The more likely culprits are a lack of exercise and an overindulgence in fat and calories.

creas either makes an inadequate amount of insulin or it makes more than enough, but the insulin isn't effectively utilized, explains diabetologist Stanley Mirsky, M.D., author of *Controlling Diabetes the Easy Way*. As with Type 1 diabetes, you end up with too much sugar in the blood.

Symptoms

• Frequent urination

• Thirst

• Blurry vision

• Tiredness

• Weight loss

• Hunger

Treatment

If left untreated, diabetes can have deadly consequences, and can wreak severe damage on the eyes, kidneys, and blood vessels.

Type 1 diabetes must be treated with insulin to keep the blood sugar level in manageable ranges.

Mild Type 2 diabetes may be controlled with diet and exercise, both of which can help your body utilize insulin better. You may also be advised to lose weight. (Up to 90 percent of people who develop Type 2 diabetes are overweight, which increases the body's resistance to insulin.)

F.Y.I.

Doctors have recently discovered that Type 2 diabetes can be delayed and even prevented. Many people who are destined to get Type 2 have higher than normal fasting blood sugar levels. By managing this "prediabetes" with diet, exercise, and sometimes drug therapy, it's possible to stall the disease and many of its complications, says Stanley Mirsky, M.D.

SMART SOURCES

National Diabetes
   Information Clearing-
   house
1 Information Way
Bethesda, MD 20892-
   3560
301-654-3327

Request consumer
publications on
diabetes.

American Diabetes
   Association
1660 Duke Street
Alexandria, VA 22314
800-342-2383
www.diabetes.org

Request free informa-
tion kits on Type 1 or
Type 2 diabetes.

If these measures don't work or your diabetes is more serious, you may need to take oral hypoglycemic drugs or even insulin shots to control your blood sugar.

Low Blood Sugar (Hypoglycemia)

Hypoglycemia is the opposite of diabetes: the body makes more insulin than it can use and takes glucose out of the blood too efficiently, leaving none to supply you with energy.

Hypoglycemia is not life threatening, but can be terribly disquieting. It can affect people who do not have diabetes, and it can affect those with diabetes if the timing of their insulin injections does not coincide with their body's needs.

Symptoms

• Weakness

• Fatigue (particularly evident before meals)

• An inability to concentrate

• Irritability

• Pale, damp skin or sweating

• Low body temperature

• Rapid heartbeat

- Shallow breathing

- Dizziness

- Sudden and/or extreme hunger

- Blurred vision

- Headache

Treatment

Eating at least three meals a day and even more frequently if you feel symptoms is the best way to avoid hypoglycemic episodes. Dr. Mirsky says you should eat a balanced diet that consists of at least 50 to 60 percent carbohydrate (the same diet prescribed for diabetics) and stringently limit your sugar intake.

Hepatitis A, B, and C

The lethal threat of viral hepatitis in the United States has reached almost epidemic proportions.

There are three forms of this dangerous virus, which can cause inflammation and scarring of the liver:

Type A, the least serious form, can be transmitted when you eat food or water that is contaminated with infected human waste. Most often this occurs because people fail to wash their hands after using the bathroom or changing a baby's diaper, and then they touch food or water. The infection

WHAT MATTERS, WHAT DOESN'T

What Matters
- Preventing physical problems by taking care of yourself and getting good health care.

- Seeking treatment if a physical or mental problem persists.

- Trying safe alternative and self-help remedies, such as exercise, as long as they don't interfere with other treatments.

- Being a proactive and informed patient.

What Doesn't
- Giving in to feelings of embarrassment about being ill (especially with anxiety or depression).

- The skill and reputation of your doctor if he or she won't listen to your concerns and let you be a partner in your health care.

- Being a passive patient and blindly following your doctor's recommendations.

usually goes away without treatment within a few months and doesn't cause long-term health effects.

Hepatitis A affects some 125,000 to 200,000 people yearly.

Type B, which can progress to chronic liver disease, scarring of the liver (cirrhosis), and pos-

Drug Side Effects

Many drugs can produce fatigue and sleepiness as a side effect. Here's a brief rundown of some common types of drugs that may make you sleepy.

- Antihistamines

- High blood pressure medicines

- Cough suppressants

- Antidiarrheals

- Antinausea drugs

- Pain relievers

- Tranquilizers

- Sleeping pills

- Headache medications

- Muscle relaxants

- Heart medications

- PMS and menstrual cramping medications

Check the label or package insert (PI)—you may have to ask your pharmacist for the latter for a prescription drug—to see if fatigue is listed as a side effect. Or look in the *Physicians' Desk Reference,* available in libraries; it contains the PIs for most prescription drugs.

sibly liver cancer, can be contracted during unprotected intercourse with a partner who is infected, or via a blood transfusion that took place before 1992 (blood supplies began to be checked then). A mother can also transmit the virus to her baby.

Hepatitis B infects 128,000 to 320,000 people annually; 1 million Americans carry the virus.

Type C, the most serious of the three hepatitis viruses, can be transmitted during unprotected sex with an infected partner or from a blood transfusion that occurred prior to 1992. The disease is usually chronic and progressive, and can lead to cirrhosis and liver cancer.

Four million people are currently infected with hepatitis C and approximately 128,000 to 180,000 new infections occur each year.

Symptoms

• May produce no recognizable symptoms

• Flulike symptoms (nausea, vomiting, fever)

• Persistent tiredness and weakness (often lasting weeks to months)

• Pain in the liver area

• Dark urine

• Light-colored stools

• Loss of appetite

• Yellow eyes and skin (jaundice)

Treatment

If you get the type A virus, your symptoms will usually resolve within six months; no treatment, other than rest, is needed.

If you get the type B virus, you also may be told simply to rest. Or you may receive an antiviral drug called alpha interferon to suppress the virus.

If you get the type C virus, you may receive a new dual-treatment regimen that combines alpha interferon and another drug called ribavarin; this combination appears to be ten times more effective in suppressing the hepatitis C virus than interferon alone.

Currently there are vaccines available to protect against the A and B hepatitis strains, but not the C type.

Overweight and Obesity

There is a direct association between your weight and your energy level: the more weight you have to carry around, the more energy your body has to exert—and the less you have left over to fuel other, less basic activities.

There's also the issue of the health effects of being overweight or obese; both increase your risk for heart disease, stroke, diabetes, high blood pressure, and cancer. And being "fat" typically negatively influences your self-esteem and your body image. Excess poundage has a deleterious effect on your pep, your health, and your quality of life.

The bad news is that many more of us may be overweight than we once thought: In June of 1998, the National Heart, Lung, and Blood Institute published a new set of weight guidelines defining healthy and unhealthy weights. As a result, about 29 million previously healthy-weight Americans were shifted into the unhealthy weight category.

The guidelines discuss healthy and unhealthy weights in terms of body mass index (BMI) rather than pounds (because, the experts say, BMI is a better indicator of "fatness" and applies to both men and women). A BMI between 18.5 and 24.9 is normal, between 25.0 and 29.9 is overweight, and over 30.0 is obese. (See the sidebar for the BMI formula.)

Symptoms

• High BMI and weight for height

• Physical discomfort

• Breathlessness

• Medical problems (diabetes and high blood pressure, among others)

Treatment

You know the drill: reduce the calories you eat and increase your exercise level. In some severe cases, diet drugs may be prescribed to help you lose weight; these medications tend to carry as many potential risks as benefits, however. Two prescription weight-loss drugs, Redux and Pondimin,

F.Y.I.

How to calculate your body mass index (BMI):

1. Multiply your weight in pounds by 704.5.

2. Multiply your height in inches by your height in inches.

3. Divide your weight calculation by your height calculation to get your BMI.

Here's an example of how a calculation would look for a man who weighs 170 pounds and is 5'10" (70 inches tall):

170 pounds x 704.5 = 119,765

70 inches x 70 inches = 4,900

119,765 ÷ 4,900 = 24.4

F.Y.I.

Although energy is intricately linked to the body, there are cases where, despite severe physical illness and disability, people are able to overcome their limitations and demonstrate a stunning energy of the mind. While their bodies shrivel and waste, their minds soar.

A classic case of mind over body is British physicist Stephen Hawking, who was diagnosed with the usually fatal nerve-wasting disorder amyotrophic lateral sclerosis (Lou Gehrig's disease). Hawking is paralyzed and unable to speak and breathe on his own. Yet he has become the top physicist of our time and has impacted the world with his "big bang" theory of the creation of the universe.

For someone so overcome with physical dysfunction, Hawking has lived, prospered, and contributed to society far beyond most healthy people's wildest dreams.

were even taken off the market in 1997 after their use was associated with heart and lung problems.

While you may have a lot of weight to lose, remember this: shedding even 10 percent of your body weight can have beneficial effects on your energy level, health, mood, and self-image.

Other Potential Energy Depleters

Vitamin Deficiency

A lack of certain vitamins in the diet is not all that common among Americans. Deficiencies tend only to occur in people with medical problems, those taking diuretics or other vitamin-sapping medications, vegetarians, and those who don't eat well (such as the elderly) or who drink too much alcohol. In these cases, improving the diet and taking the appropriate supplements will usually restore energy (assuming any underlying medical problems are corrected as well).

Recent Illness

Colds and flus are notorious for sapping energy, but usually exert only temporary effects. A bout of pneumonia can be harder to overcome, especially as you age. Major illnesses and surgeries may require major recuperation time before you get back your pep.

Checking Up on Your Physical Health

The U.S. Preventive Services Task Force advises healthy adults to have a physical exam—a checkup—every one to three years and annually after age sixty-five.

Whatever type of doctor you select to perform your exam, it's a good idea to seek out someone who is trained and interested in prevention. "Many doctors don't take prevention seriously," says Paul Frankel, M.D., Ph.D., president of Life Extension Institute, a New York City group of preventive health care specialists. "They feel they are there to treat illness." One way to tell if a doctor is prevention-oriented is to inquire if he or she is board-certified in the field by the American Board of Preventive Medicine. Another is simply to ask how strongly the doctor feels about preventive tests and procedures and what general recommendations he or she gives.

As a savvy health care consumer, you may also need to encourage your doctor to do certain exams and tests he or she might omit, or forego other evaluations he or she may think necessary. "You have to be well-educated so you'll know what represents too much care versus too little care," advises Dr. Frankel. Which is not to say that you shouldn't give credence to your personal sense of how thorough an exam you need and want to feel healthy; some people prefer to submit to frequent, extensive testing so they can have peace of mind, while others would rather not bother.

"The precise components of the exam should be tailored to your individual health risks and problems," adds Julie Abbott, M.D., chair of the Division of Preventive Medicine at the Mayo Clinic in Rochester, Minnesota. "Every time you have a physical exam, update your doctor about your family history of disease, your personal medical history, and your habits. Armed with your answers, the doctor can then counsel you about ways to modify your health risks—stop smoking, exercise more, practice safe sex," she says. Be honest and straightforward—and if counseling isn't forthcoming, request guidance. Ask, for instance, "Is there anything I could be doing for my health that I'm not?" You may not always like the answer, but at least you'll be informed.

Food Allergies

Some health experts believe that food allergies are responsible for a large number of health problems, including fatigue.

Mononucleosis

This illness is caused by the Epstein-Barr virus and is often called the "kissing disease." By the age of five, half of us have already had "mono"—often without ever knowing it. Teenagers are most prone to developing symptoms, which include tiredness, weakness, fever, and swollen glands. Bed rest for two to three weeks usually cures it.

Chronic, Low-Grade Infections

Any infection (such as sinus or urinary tract maladies) requires your body to mount an attack to fight it, which takes valuable energy. Your body's resources become even more depleted and compromised when infections recur.

Smoking

Smoking cigarettes adversely affects the delivery of oxygen to your body's tissues, which causes fatigue.

We're now ready to move on to strategies for boosting your energy level. In chapter 4, we'll look at one of the biggest factors: a healthy diet.

THE BOTTOM LINE

Fatigue is a common complaint among Americans and can be a component of any number of physical and mental illnesses: depression, anxiety, hypothyroidism, vitamin and iron deficiencies, obesity, diabetes, sleep deprivation, chronic pain syndromes, low-grade infections, drug side effects, and chronic fatigue syndrome.

Fatigue that lasts longer than three weeks, is worsening, and/or interferes with your lifestyle should be evaluated by your physician.

....

Nutrition and Energy

Few things are as elemental to energy as food. Food is the fuel on which the body runs. Without it, the body dies. With it, the body and mind can thrive.

Unfortunately, surveys consistently suggest that most Americans aren't getting the nutrition we need—and we're particularly bad about eating fruits, vegetables, grains, and dairy products. We're over the top, however, when it comes to consumption of health-risky fats, oils, and sweets.

How the Body Uses Food as Fuel

There are three main energy-producing nutrients in foods: carbohydrates, proteins, and fats. These are known as macronutrients, and most foods contain more than one. Foods also contain water, vitamins and minerals (micronutrients), and non-nutrients, such as fiber.

Current government recommendations suggest that we eat a diet that contains about 60 to 65 percent carbohydrate, 10 to 15 percent protein, and 30 percent or less fat.

Carbohydrates

Sugars and starches—carbohydrates—provide the most direct and fastest form of energy for the human body.

Simple carbohydrates or sugars include fruits, berries, certain vegetables, honey, sugars (table and brown), and the lactose in milk.

Complex carbohydrates or starches include rice, grains, cereals, beans, and starchy vegetables such as potatoes, yams, corn, and squash.

All carbohydrates are broken down into glucose, the body's main source of fuel. Glucose swims in the bloodstream until the hormone insulin escorts it into the cells, where it is burned for energy. If there is more glucose than is needed, the leftover portion is stored in the muscles and liver as glycogen and reserved for later use. If there's still glucose left over after all the glycogen stores are full, the rest of the glucose is converted to and stored as fat.

The bloodstream can hold enough glucose to fuel the body for about an hour, and the liver and muscles can store a half day's supply of glycogen. Once glucose and glycogen are used up—which can happen within a day's time—fat stores are burned for energy. After that, protein is used.

Simple carbohydrates are easier and faster for the body to break down than are complex carbohydrates. That's why simple sugars—like a candy bar—give you a quick spurt of energy. Complex carbohydrates—such as a slice of bread—offer more sustained energy because it takes the body a longer time to convert them into glucose.

An added benefit: all carbohydrates contain the amino acid tryptophan, which prompts the release of the brain chemical serotonin. Serotonin induces calm, relaxed feelings, reduces anxiety, and makes you feel drowsy.

SMART DEFINITION

Calorie

The energy contained in food. Specific calorie counts are determined by calculating the amount of heat generated by a food when it is burned in a calorimeter, a laboratory device that simulates the human body's metabolic process.

DON'T SKIP BREAKFAST!

Skipping breakfast can be a top reason for a lack of energy—and an excess of weight. "If you have dinner at 6 P.M., your body will have digested that food by the time you wake up the next morning," notes Mark Meskin, Ph.D., R.D., professor of food, nutrition, and consumer sciences at California State Polytechnic University in Pomona, California. "If you don't eat breakfast, you'll be running on empty at the very time of day (mid-morning) when your circadian rhythms are peaking. Thus, you'll be cheating yourself out of your optimal energy period."

Forgoing breakfast also sets you up for hunger pangs later in the morning. At that point, you're apt to reach for something fast, fattening, and low in nutrients (say a muffin or doughnut and a cup of coffee).

"If you're not hungry when you first wake up, you don't have to fight it," says Tammy Baker, M.S., R.D., a spokesperson for the American Dietetic Association. "Try having a glass of juice or milk and a low-fat granola bar to tide your body over until you're more ready to eat," she suggests. Then, opt for a piece of fruit or half a bagel from the coffee cart—not a Danish!

Protein

Protein is composed of amino acids and is essential to many bodily functions, including the production of insulin and the transporting of nutrients and oxygen through the bloodstream and around the body. Common protein sources include red meat, poultry, fish, eggs, dairy products, legumes, soy products, and nuts.

Protein is a poor third to carbohydrates and fats as a direct energy source; the body tends to burn it only when you aren't eating enough of the other nutrients. On the other hand, if you take in more protein than you can use, just like carbohydrates and fats, it is stored as glycogen or fat for later energy use.

Although protein isn't used as a primary energy source, it serves as an energy booster nonetheless. The reason: protein contains the amino acid tyrosine, which spurs the synthesis of the brain chemicals nor-epinephrine and dopamine. These chemicals keep you alert and motivated, improve your reaction time, and boost both physical and mental energy levels. They also tend to overpower the serotonin released in response to carbohydrate consumption. That's why dietitians recommend eating a little protein with your carbohydrates at breakfast and lunch; the carbs will give you immediate energy, and the protein will help sustain that energy by stimulating the release of dopamine and norepinephrine.

Fats

Common fats include oils, shortening, lard, butter, margarine, mayonnaise, cream, and fats found in meat and poultry.

Fats have a bad reputation, but they're actually as critical to our body's survival as are protein and carbohydrates. There are certain types of fats—essential fatty acids—you can only get from foods, and that are needed to perform important bodily functions. Also, you need fats to absorb vitamins A, D, E, and K. The problem is Americans eat too many fats, which increases the risk of heart disease, cancer, and many other health problems.

Fats take the longest time to digest of the three macronutrients because they are the most calorically dense. (They contain nine calories per gram, whereas protein and carbohydrates contain

F.Y.I.

How quickly does blood sugar rise when you eat carbohydrates as compared to protein and fat? Elizabeth Somer, M.A., R.D., author of *Food and Mood: The Complete Guide to Eating Well and Feeling Your Best*, offers this assessment:

• **After eating simple sugars** your blood sugar rises within ten to fifteen minutes to a level above normal; within twenty-five to forty-five minutes later, it crashes to a level below normal.

• **After eating starches** your blood sugar level slowly and steadily increases for up to four hours.

• **After eating protein and fat** your blood sugar level stabilizes for up to four hours.

SMART SOURCES

To subscribe to great nutrition newsletters:

Environmental Nutrition
P.O. Box 420451
Palm Coast, FL
    32142-0451
800-829-5384
$30 for 12 issues a
    year

*Nutrition Action Health
    Letter*
Center for Science in
    the Public Interest
1875 Connecticut
    Avenue, NW, Suite
    300
Washington, D.C.
    20009-5728
www.cspinet.org
$24 for 10 issues a
    year

*Tufts University Health
    & Nutrition Letter*
P.O. Box 57857
Boulder, CO 80322-
    7857
800-274-7581
$24 for 12 issues a
    year

only four calories per gram.) The extended digestion process diverts energy away from other bodily functions, making you feel sluggish.

Although your body first relies on carbohydrates—in the form of glucose and glycogen—for energy during any form of physical activity, after about twenty to thirty minutes it starts to dip into its fat stores. Endurance athletes inevitably use fats to fuel them during their extended bouts of exercise. Dieters also may eat up some of their fat stores, but only if they take in fewer calories than their bodies need to maintain weight.

An Energy-Boosting Diet

The following is meant to provide you with a road map to smart, energy-enhancing, daily meals.

Breakfast: Eat mostly carbohydrates in the morning to provide you with instant energy. Balance that, though, with some protein to prevent the drowsiness that carbohydrates can induce. A small bagel with a slice of low-fat melted cheese, cereal with low-fat milk and fruit, or low-fat yogurt with a low-fat muffin are good choices.

Mid-morning: Have a piece of fruit and some low-fat yogurt to tide you over until lunchtime.

Lunchtime: For this meal, mix protein with carbohydrates—and keep this meal light. Carbohydrates alone may make you crash and burn even worse than if you hadn't eaten at all (because of the serotonin release), but mixed with a little protein will provide both a short- and long-term energy boost. Try turkey or tuna salad with fresh vegetables on grain bread (nix the heavy mayonnaise for a light mayo or lemon juice), or pasta with a little ham and oil-and-vinegar dressing.

Also, don't start any meal with bread. Massachusetts Institute of Technology research scientist Judith Wurtman, Ph.D., who has pioneered research in the field of food, energy, and mood, says that eating bread first will release tryptophan (and serotonin) and make you drowsy. Instead, start with salad, juice, or consommé.

Midafternoon: If you're prone to carbohydrate cravings, have a snack of crackers, fruit, or starchy vegetables to offset the postlunch slump.

Dinner: Go easy on your intake of fat and carbohydrates, because they'll make you feel sleepy. Instead emphasize foods with protein—fish, lean cuts of meat, low-fat cheese—so you'll have energy for evening activities. That doesn't give you the go-ahead to forego vegetables; just go light on them and eat them after your protein.

Half an hour to two hours before bed: Have some carbohydrates, to induce sleepiness. Graham crackers or other types of low-fat cookies are also good options.

Important: If you're looking for high energy, don't eat more than five hundred calories per meal, advises dietitian Tammy Baker. "When you eat a big meal, more blood pools to the stomach and away from the brain to aid in digestion. That makes you sluggish." There's also evidence that

SMART MOVE

You may have seen advertisements hawking liquid nutrition drinks—Ensure, Boost—not just to older adults but to active younger people, too. Are they a good buy or just a gimmick? Nutrition experts are divided.

On the pro side, energy drinks are convenient, and they contain the recommended daily allowances for many nutrients. They're high in energy-boosting carbohydrates, too. So if you're apt to skip a meal or to eat junk food, these shakes will give you a nutrient and energy boost to take you through to your next meal of the day.

On the con side, the drinks don't contain many of the complex nutrients found in whole foods, such as phytochemicals. They can also be costly and their taste can leave something to be desired. Plus they pack about 250 calories per serving.

the body can't digest more than five hundred calories at a time, so eating high-calorie meals will only increase your chances of gaining fat.

Water Works

The value of water in a healthy diet can't be underestimated. It's actually the most important nutrient of all: the body is largely composed of water, uses water to perform almost every bodily function, and can't go for more than a few days without a new supply.

The human body excretes about two and a half to three quarts of water a day. That water needs to be replaced by drinking liquids that contain water, as well as by consuming fruits and vegetables (which are 80 to 95 percent water) and other foods. If it isn't, dehydration results with symptoms such as fatigue, weakness, dizziness, and headache.

By the way, thirst isn't a good indicator of your need for water. "If you're thirsty, you've already lost a couple of cups of water from the body," says Tammy Baker. She recommends drinking eight 8-ounce glasses of water per day—and even more when you're exercising.

Why Grazing Pays

Eating small meals every three to four hours, know as grazing, is a good energy-boosting strategy because it avoids the spikes and valleys in your blood sugar that can cause fatigue. You're also less likely to be ravenously hungry at any one meal if you're grazing—and thus you'll be less likely to overeat. (Of course, your food choices matter, too, but if you keep to low-fat, low-to-moderate-calorie meals you should do fine.)

Why Candy, Coffee, and Alcohol Don't Pay

Sugars

Although simple sugars—candy, doughnuts, cookies—offer a quick energy payoff, the boost is only temporary. In response to a candy bar, your blood sugar level will rise dramatically and quickly—and you'll feel it. But within about an hour, the insulin released to clear the sugar from the bloodstream will have done its job, leaving you with lower blood sugar levels than before you ate.

As a carbohydrate, sugar also triggers the release of serotonin, the calming brain chemical, so you'll have to contend with those effects, too. That's no small feat, since serotonin's influence can last for up to three and a half hours after a candy bar snack.

If you frequently rely on candy to fuel you, you're not getting the other nutrients you need to keep your body strong and healthy. And you're using a quick fix for a problem that probably has deep-seated causes—such as a lack of good nutrition, sleep, or exercise.

A better choice for a quick fix is fruit—be it an apple, pear, banana, melon, whatever. "Fruit, although a simple sugar, contains fiber, which slows down the release of glucose into the blood stream,"

F.Y.I.

Why do we crave sweets? "We're built that way," says William V. Tamborlane, M.D., professor of pediatrics at Yale University School of Medicine in New Haven, Connecticut.

The human tongue has a desire to sample all food tastes at every meal: sweet, sour, bitter, and salty. "Even after we're full, we may have a yearning for dessert if we didn't have anything sweet during a meal," he says. Instead of denying your sweet tooth, then, indulge it . . . in moderation. (There's always fruit! And there's nothing wrong with a cookie or two.)

F.Y.I.

Other sources of caffeine:

Tea

Soft drinks

Chocolate (including hot cocoa and chocolate milk)

Some medications (especially those for headache)

explains Baker. "That way, you get a more sustained energy boost."

Coffee

Coffee may be second only to soft drinks as the top beverage choice in the United States, but that doesn't make it the ideal energy boost. It's true that the caffeine in coffee is stimulating; that's because it inhibits the brain chemical adenosine, which can make you feel tired. But drinking too much coffee can actually have a rebound effect, and also *make* you tired: after one cup, you get the initial high and a rise in blood sugar, just as with a candy bar, but then you slump again within about an hour, as your blood sugar falls to a level below normal. That prompts you to drink more coffee. . . and sets you up for a vicious cycle of increasing coffee consumption to combat daytime drowsiness.

One to three cups of coffee a day (up to 300 milligrams of caffeine) consumed before the mid-afternoon is considered okay; more than that, and you're setting yourself up for trouble (dependence and withdrawal headaches if you don't drink enough, as well as fatigue). Drinking coffee in the late afternoon or evening is also a no-no, especially if you're sensitive to the effects of caffeine, because it can impair sleep.

One further caveat: you may think you're getting more than enough water because coffee contains that very liquid—but ironically the reverse is true. Coffee is actually a diuretic, so by drinking several cups a day you're robbing your body of needed fluids and contributing to energy depletion. At the very least, compensate for your coffee consumption by stepping up your intake of water.

Alcohol

Drinking a cocktail or two can give you an initial kick, but it's all downhill from there. Like coffee, alcohol is a diuretic, so you're losing fluids when you drink it. It also inhibits the body's absorption of energy-essential B vitamins and may increase your appetite. And though it may seem to help you sleep well early in the night, when its effects wear off later you're apt to wake up and have trouble getting back to sleep. Current recommendations suggest that men should restrict daily alcohol intake to two drinks a day, and women to one drink a day.

"In general, stimulants like caffeine and alcohol borrow energy from the future," explains Laurie Meyer, R.D., a nutrition consultant in private practice in Milwaukee, Wisconsin. "You may get some temporary pep, but it's really a false kind of energy. And it ultimately sets you up to crash."

Also Avoid: Refined and Processed Foods

Refined foods are foods that have been changed from their natural state, losing many nutrients in the process. White flour and white rice, which have had the outer layer of grain removed, are prime examples of refined foods.

Processed foods are those that have been changed during manufacturing to purify them, make them more palatable, or make them last longer on the shelf. Chips, cookies, soups, and ready-made meals are common processed foods; they've been altered from their natural state to

STREET SMARTS

Up until a few years ago, Hildy, thirty-nine, a medical project planner, relied on an afternoon candy bar and a Coke to pick her up after lunch. "My coworkers used to joke in the afternoon when they'd find me away from desk—which was strewn with candy bar wrappers, soda cans, and cigarettes—that I was either in the bathroom or dead," she recalls.

These days Hildy is much more health conscious—and has more energy as a result. "I still eat candy on occasion, but I'm much more apt to reach for a piece of fruit and pretzels as an afternoon snack because I don't tend to spike and then crash as much," she says.

F.Y.I.

To calculate your daily fat gram budget according to the government's 30 percent rule, use this formula:

Multiply your total number of daily calories by 0.30 and then divide by 9. If you're eating 2,200 calories a day, the calculation would work out like this:

2,200 calories x 0.30 = 660 calories from fat ÷ 9 grams = 73 grams of fat.

Keep track of your fat gram intake by consulting food labels and fat counters.

create boxed, canned, packaged, and plastic-wrapped food products. Oftentimes, processing strips nutrients from foods and adds unwanted fat, sodium, and preservatives. Some nutrients may be added back in—as when foods are fortified—but yet-to-be identified healthy compounds lost in the manufacturing process can never be replaced.

"The closer to the natural state a food is, the greater its nutritional value," says Tammy Baker. And the more oomph it will give you.

The Dietary Guidelines for Americans

The Dietary Guidelines for Americans, last published in December 1995, are the U.S. Department of Agriculture's recommendations for healthy eating.

Although everyone has different food needs based on their gender, age, genetics, and how active they are, these guidelines emphasize a low-fat, low-to-moderate-protein, high-carbohydrate diet as the healthiest food plan for most Americans to follow.

There are seven major recommendations in the Dietary Guidelines for Americans. They are:

• **Eat a variety of foods.** Varying your food choices to include grains, fruits, vegetables, dairy products, meat, poultry, fish, beans, lentils, fats, and sweets will provide you with all of the vitamins, minerals, and other nutrients you need to stay healthy and maintain a high energy level.

• **Balance the food you eat with physical activity, and maintain or improve your weight.** Carrying excess weight is a health risk—most recently, the American Heart Association listed obesity as an independent risk factor for heart disease, like smoking, high blood pressure, and a high cholesterol level. Obesity also raises the risk for stroke, diabetes, cancer, arthritis, and breathing disorders. Some research suggests that even small weight gains with age can be deleterious to your health—and most Americans do get heavier as they get older.

• **Choose a diet with plenty of grains, vegetables, and fruits.** Base all of your meals on these foods, which contain lots of vitamins, minerals, complex carbohydrates, and other healthy compounds, and tend to be low in fat.

• **Choose a diet low in fat, saturated fat, and cholesterol.** Keep fat intake to 30 percent or less of your total daily calories. (See sidebar on page 72 to figure out how many fat grams you can safely eat per day.)

• **Choose a diet moderate in sugars.** Most Americans eat far too much sugar, which is high in calories and tends to pack on weight.

• **Choose a diet moderate in salt.** Our diets also tend to be high in salt, which is associated with an increased risk for high blood pressure. Large amounts of salt are contained in processed and prepared foods.

• **If you drink alcoholic beverages, do so in moderation.** Although research suggests that limited

SMART SOURCES

United States Department of Agriculture (USDA)
202-208-2417

Ask for the *Dietary Guidelines for Americans* (Home and Garden Bulletin No. 232) and the *Food Guide Pyramid* (Home and Garden Bulletin No. 252).

American Dietetic Association
ADAF-GNRL
P.O. Box 77-6034
Chicago, IL 60678-6034

For the *Good Nutrition Reading List,* a guide to consumer books and newsletters, send $3.50 and a self-addressed, stamped, business-size envelope.

American Dietetic Association Consumer Nutrition Line
800-366-1655
(weekdays 10 A.M. to 4 P.M.)

Speak to registered dietitians and hear recorded nutrition messages.

amounts of alcohol may have some beneficial health effects, alcohol is lacking in nutrients, contains a lot of calories, and is linked with a number of diseases when overconsumed.

The Food Guide Pyramid

In 1992, the Food Guide Pyramid was revised to assist Americans in putting the Dietary Guidelines for Americans into practice. "Along with the guidelines, the Food Guide Pyramid is a good place to start if you're trying to be healthier and boost energy," says dietitian Laurie Meyer.

There are four levels to the Food Guide Pyramid (see illustration on the next page):

• The bottom rung consists of the bread, cereal, rice, and pasta group (complex carbohydrates). You should consume six to eleven servings of these foods per day and include them in every meal. Grains and other complex carbohydrates contain fiber, vitamins, and minerals—and lots of energy.

• The next level up houses the fruit and vegetable groups. Try to get two to four servings of fruits and three to five servings of vegetables a day. Most Americans fall short in eating fruits and vegetables, which are great sources of vitamins, minerals, and fiber.

• The third rung contains the meat, poultry, fish, dry beans, eggs, and nut group. You should limit your intake of these foods to two to three servings

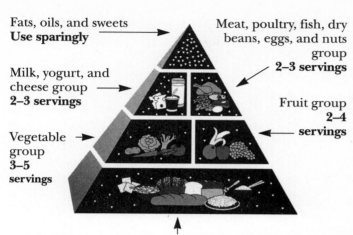

Fats, oils, and sweets **Use sparingly**

Meat, poultry, fish, dry beans, eggs, and nuts group **2–3 servings**

Milk, yogurt, and cheese group **2–3 servings**

Fruit group **2–4 servings**

Vegetable group **3–5 servings**

Bread, cereal, rice, and pasta group **6–11 servings**

Source: U.S. Department of Agriculture

a day. (Although high in protein, these foods can also be high in fat.) The milk, yogurt, and cheese group is also on this level. Strive to consume two to three servings a day of these foods, important sources of protein, calcium, iron, and zinc.

• The upper rung contains the fats, oils, and sweets group. You should eat these foods "sparingly." Your body requires a little fat to perform metabolic processes, but most Americans eat way too many fatty, high-calorie foods to stay healthy and maintain an appropriate weight.

Calorie Counts

Both overeating and undereating can sap vitality: overeating adds pounds, making your body epend more energy to perform metabolic processes and to move; undereating, by subtly starving the body.

Here are the USDA daily recommended calorie counts for various groups of people:

WHAT MATTERS, WHAT DOESN'T

What Matters

• Eating frequently (at least three meals a day).

• Eating real food, not refined or processed food.

• Eating a well-balanced diet, containing complex carbohydrates, protein, and fat.

• Sticking to appropriate portion sizes.

• Drinking water.

What Doesn't

• Fad "protein" and other diets.

• Consuming nutrition drinks or energy bars.

• Eating food in certain sequences or combinations (such as not eating fruit with other foods and not mixing proteins at a single meal, as some trendy diets dictate).

Serving Sizes

As with most things American, our food portions tend to be huge. Our national motto seems to be, "the bigger, the better." But research shows that moderation in most things is best—and that's true for food, as much as for anything else in life.

You may think that the Food Guide Pyramid's suggestions that you eat six to eleven servings of grains and three to five servings of vegetables a day are right in keeping with that "bigger is better" philosophy. But take a look at how a true portion sizes up, and you'll see huge isn't in—and meeting the government's guidelines may not be as tough as it sounds.

Bread, Cereal, Rice, Pasta

- 1 slice of bread

- 1 ounce of ready-to-eat cold cereal

- ½ cup of cooked cereal, rice, or pasta

Vegetables

- 1 cup of raw leafy vegetables

- ½ cup of other types of vegetables, cooked or raw

- ¾ cup of vegetable juice

Fruits

- 1 medium apple, banana, orange, pear, or other fruit

- ½ cup of chopped, cooked, or canned fruit

- ¾ cup of fruit juice

Milk, Yogurt, Cheese

- 1 cup of milk or yogurt

- 1½ ounce of natural cheese

- 2 ounce of processed cheese

Meat, Poultry, Fish, Dry Beans, Eggs, Nuts

- 2–3 ounces of cooked lean meat, poultry, or fish

- ½ cup of cooked dry beans

NOTE: 1 egg, 2 tablespoons peanut butter, or ⅓ cup nuts = 1 ounce lean meat

• If you're a sedentary woman or an older adult, aim to eat approximately 1,600 calories a day. Limit your fat intake to 53 grams, and your added sugars to 6 teaspoons.

• If you're a child, teenage girl, active woman, or a sedentary man, consume about 2,200 calories a day. Restrict yourself to 73 grams of fat and 12 teaspoons of added sugars.

• If you're a teenage boy, an active man, or a very active woman, you can eat 2,800 calories a day, 93 grams of fat, and 18 teaspoons of added sugars.

Food Pyramid Checklist

Copy this page and circle the number of servings from each category you consume daily. The recommended numbers are listed in parentheses next to each food group.

Food Group	Number of Servings										
Breads, Cereal, Rice, Pasta	1	2	3	4	5	6	7	8	9	10	11
Vegetables (3–5)	1	2	3	4	5	6	7	8	9	10	11
Fruits (2–4)	1	2	3	4	5	6	7	8	9	10	11
Milk, Yogurt, Cheese (2–3)	1	2	3	4	5	6	7	8	9	10	11
Meat, Poultry, Fish, Dry Beans, Eggs, Nuts (2–3)	1	2	3	4	5	6	7	8	9	10	11
Fats, Oils, Sweets (use sparingly)	1	2	3	4	5	6	7	8	9	10	11

Assessment for the day:

Under   On Target   Over

The "Fat Instinct" Explained

As director of the Pritikin Longevity Centers in Miami and Santa Monica—and son of the great nutritional expert Dr. Nathan Pritikin—Robert Pritikin knows how hard it is to follow a healthy diet and control cravings for fatty foods. In his book *The Pritikin Weight Loss Breakthrough,* he describes how humans developed what he calls the "fat instinct."

"The fat instinct is a basic survival mechanism that dates back to our days as cavemen, when the food supply was unpredictable," he explains. "Hunger was the primary nutritional concern, so whenever they could, our ancestors ate foods that had a high concentration of calories. The best source was fat, which contains nine calories per gram."

Fast-forward to modern times: our food supply is highly predictable today, yet most of us still crave and eat fat whenever we can, and don't exercise. "As a result, half of the U.S. population is obese," he says.

How do you overcome the fat instinct? Pritikin's five-pronged plan has helped some seventy thousand people lose weight over the past twenty years:

- **Eat frequent meals and snacks to raise your metabolic rate and burn more calories.** He recommends eating three main meals—two of which shouldn't contain meat—in addition to small snacks at mid-morning and mid-afternoon.

- **Choose healthy, low-fat, carbohydrate-rich foods such as fruits, vegetables, and grains that make you feel full quickly, so you'll eat less.** The body has a limited capacity for storing carbohydrates, so they fill you up quickly with a minimum of calories. (In contrast, the body has an unlimited capacity for storing fat.)

- **Exercise regularly.** Exercise exerts influence over what you eat because it burns up your limited stores of carbohydrates. "After exercise, you'll actually crave fruit rather than fat because your body will need to replenish those reserves," says Pritikin. Regular exercise will also help you build and maintain lean muscle mass, which in turn will help you burn a greater number of calories.

- **Go light on fat, so you'll crave it less.** Limit it to 30 percent or fewer of your daily calories.

- **Be consistent.** Everyone slips up now and then and succumbs to fatty foods. But the more you restrict your indulgences, the better you'll keep your fat instinct under lock and key.

For Vegetarians Only

If you don't eat meat, you probably have a one-up on the others who do: vegetarians are typically big fruit, vegetable, and grain eaters. But you must be sure to devise other ways to get the minimum recommended amounts of protein, iron, zinc, and B vitamins—usually obtained from meat—that your body needs to perform metabolic processes and continue producing energy.

Likewise, if you're not eating dairy products, you need to identify foods that offer the protein, calcium, and vitamin D others get from eating milk, eggs, cheese, and yogurt.

To compensate, you might rely on soy protein (tofu, tempeh, soy milk), fortified foods, dark green leafy vegetables, legumes, nuts, and other plant-source nutrients. You might also consider taking a daily multivitamin/mineral supplement.

It sounds strange, but you've got to expend energy to make energy. So, that's what we'll cover in chapter 5: exercise.

THE BOTTOM LINE

A balanced array of foods from the carbohydrate, protein, and fat families are needed to fuel the body and create energy. Based on extensive scientific research, the government recommends limiting fat intake to 30 percent of total daily calories, and increasing consumption of grains, fruits, vegetables, and low-fat dairy products.

Carbohydrates are the body's preferred energy sources, and produce fast but fleeting energy; they can also make you drowsy, since they cause the release of the brain chemical serotonin. Combining carbohydrates with protein provides more sustained energy, because protein prompts the release of two brain chemicals that foster alertness— and overpower the effects of serotonin.

Exercise and Energy

Have you ever noticed that when you feel pooped, if you push yourself and get moving, you get that resurgence of pep, but if you give in, you just feel more tired? The reason: Exercise stimulates the body and the mind.

"There's lots of evidence that exercise is beneficial for energy," reports Michael Scholtz, M.A., fitness director for the Duke University Diet & Fitness Center in Durham, North Carolina. Most of us know that physical activity helps to maintain weight, enhances sleep, improves immunity, and wards off a number of serious health ailments, such as cancer, diabetes, high blood pressure, and osteoporosis (bone thinning that occurs with age). "But exercise also reduces anxiety, stress, and other factors that can draw energy away from you, and improves your mood," he says.

"The mood-boosting effects of exercise are so powerful that nine out of ten people say that's what motivates them to keep with it," adds Kenneth Cooper, M.D., M.P.H. (head of the Cooper Aerobics Center in Dallas, Texas, and the man who coined the term "aerobics" back in 1968).

Guidelines for Good Health—and Energy

American adults are a sedentary bunch: 60 percent aren't active on a regular basis, and a quarter are completely sedentary (see pie chart on page 83). Studies show that inactive people have double the risk for coronary heart disease compared with physically active people.

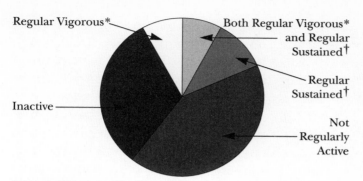

Regular Vigorous*

Inactive

Both Regular Vigorous*
and Regular
Sustained†

Regular
Sustained†

Not
Regularly
Active

* Regular Vigorous=20 minutes 3 times per week of vigorous intensity

† Regular Sustained=30 minutes 5 times per week of any intensity

Source: CDC 1992 Behavioral Risk Factor Survey

The Centers for Disease Control report that only about a quarter of Americans are active on a regular basis. The rest of us are, well, sloths, and 25 percent don't get any exercise at all.

In 1978, the American College of Sports Medicine (ACSM) released exercise guidelines for Americans: these guidelines stated that adults should work out for fifteen to sixty minutes three to five times a week at a vigorous pace that raises the heart rate to between 60 and 90 percent of its maximum. Most Americans pretty much ignored the recommendations. Even though most people were aware of the health benefits of exercise, they weren't convinced it was worth the effort or they couldn't find the time to do it.

All in Moderation

To combat our lack of enthusiasm for exercise, the Centers for Disease Control (CDC), the U.S. Surgeon General's Office, and the ACSM devised exercise "lite" guidelines in 1993. These relaxed guidelines call for all Americans to accumulate

Moderate exercise

Brisk activity that makes you breathe a little more quickly, but not so much that you're out of breath. ("Slightly winded" is a favored term in "exercise lite" circles.) The activity should burn about 4.5 calories a minute. If you're walking, you should keep up a 3 to 4.5 mph pace.

thirty minutes or more of moderate intensity physical activity on most days of the week. Although it's most desirable to perform the activity all at once, it can also be broken up into ten- to fifteen-minute sessions with much the same effect.

Walking is commonly cited as the best form of moderate exercise, but everyday activities will also suffice: gardening, washing a car, walking the dog, shoveling snow, and climbing stairs count toward your daily total, as long as you keep moving.

Moderate activity can provide substantial health benefits. In fact, you reap more benefits by going from a sedentary state to a moderately active state than you do going from being moderately active to being vigorously active. Research at the Cooper Aerobics Center indicates that progressing from a sedentary lifestyle to exercising at a moderate intensity reduces the risk of death from any cause by 58 percent over a ten-year period and adds two and a half years to the life span.

Moderate lifestyle exercise can even burn as many calories as more many traditional, organized activity. Another Cooper Aerobics Center study of 235 volunteers found that moderate exercisers who incorporated physical activity into their everyday lives burned as many calories—an average of 159 per day—and gained as much muscle and lost as much fat as did gym-goers who exercised more intensely.

Examples of Moderate Amounts of Activity

Washing and waxing a car for 45–60 minutes

Washing windows or floors for 45–60 minutes

Playing volleyball for 45 minutes

Playing touch football for 30–45 minutes

Gardening for 30–45 minutes

Wheeling self in wheelchair for 30–40 minutes

Walking 1¾ miles in 35 minutes (20 min./mile)

Basketball (shooting baskets) for 30 minutes

Bicycling 5 miles in 30 minutes

Dancing fast (social) for 30 minutes

Pushing a stroller 1½ miles in 15 minutes (10 min./mile)

Raking leaves for 30 minutes

Walking 2 miles in 30 minutes (15 min./mile)

Water aerobics for 30 minutes

Swimming laps for 20 minutes

Wheelchair basketball for 20 minutes

Basketball (playing a game) for 15–20 minutes

Bicycling 4 miles in 15 minutes

Jumping rope for 15 minutes

Running 1½ miles in 15 minutes (10 min./mile)

Shoveling snow for 15 minutes

Stairwalking for 15 minutes

Less Vigorous, More Time

↑
|
|
↓

More Vigorous, Less Time

Source: At-A-Glance companion document to *Physical Activity and Health: A Report of the Surgeon General,* Centers for Disease Control and Prevention

Vigorous (Aerobic) Exercise

While moderate exercise will definitely give you more zip, if you're looking to gain the kind of energy and stamina you need to play three sets of single's tennis or run a minimarathon, you're going to have to up the intensity of your workout to an aerobic level—and sustain it there for at least twenty minutes at a time. (We're talking sweat.)

It's paradoxical, but the more energy you expend, the more energy you'll have and vice versa. "To become aerobically fit, you have to overload your cardiovascular system so it adapts to a greater workload," explains James Rippe, M.D., director of the Center for Clinical and Lifestyle Research in Shrewsbury, Massachusetts. Your heart has to get stronger, so it will pump more oxygen to your muscles; in turn, that will allow your muscles to become more efficient in converting fuel into energy. Scholtz adds that "The fitter you are, the less effort it takes to do something. It's like having a bigger-than-usual engine in a small car."

Sustained, intense activity is critical to pushing yourself to an aerobically fit level. Scholtz recommends exercising for twenty to thirty minutes three to five times a week, at a heart rate that is between 70 to 90 percent of your maximal rate. Good activities to try include running, aerobic dancing, skating, rowing, cycling, cross-country skiing, swimming, stairclimbing, and racewalking.

"Don't expect overnight results; it can take six weeks to feel the effects," he says. And if you stop exercising, within weeks you will lose the benefits you've gained. That means you've got to commit to a regimen.

Good Exercise Practices

To prime your body for exercise and reduce the risk of injury, follow these guidelines:

Warm Up and Stretch

Warm up for three to five minutes using the muscles you'll be working during your session. If you're planning to run, walk at a brisk pace for a quarter mile. If you're bike riding, pedal in a low gear first.

Next, for three to four minutes, stretch the body parts you'll be using. Stretching is important because it makes your muscles more flexible. It also feels good. But proper technique is critical: Don't stretch so much that it hurts. Instead, pull out the muscle until you feel slight tension; then hold the position for ten to thirty seconds. Relax, and then repeat the stretch. Don't bounce while stretching, either; stay still to avoid injury.

Exercise

How long you exercise depends on your goals, your fitness level, and how much time you have. For aerobic benefits, remember that the ACSM says you need to exercise for at least fifteen minutes at 60 to 90 percent of your maximum heart rate (not including the warm-up and cool-down).

If you're going for a moderate-intensity workout, shoot to burn 4.5 calories a minute or walk at a 3 to 4.5 mile-per-hour pace.

F.Y.I.

To figure out your maximum heart rate—get out your calculator—subtract your age from 220 and take a percentage of that figure. If your age is 35 and you're trying to work out at 80 percent of your maximum heart rate, the calculation would look like this: 220 − 35 = 185 x 80 percent = 148 beats per minute (bpm).

Cool Down and Stretch Again

As vital to a good workout as the warm-up and the exercise itself is the cooling down and stretching of your muscles after a session. Done properly, this lessens your risk of serious injury and muscle soreness. Walk slowly for five minutes after exercise to help your body adjust to the lesser demands on it.

The Cooper Clinic's Walking Tips

Kenneth Cooper, M.D., M.P.H., has created a six-week basic walking program for his patients at the Cooper Aerobics Center that meets the government's guidelines for moderate activity. (Each week calls for five walks.)

- **Week 1:** Walk one mile in twenty-four minutes.

- **Week 2:** Walk one mile in twenty-two minutes.

- **Week 3:** Walk one mile in twenty minutes.

- **Week 4:** Walk one and a half miles in thirty minutes.

- **Week 5:** Walk one and a half miles in twenty-nine minutes.

- **Week 6:** Walk two miles in under forty minutes.

   If you want to progress to a more vigorous workout after you finish the six weeks of basic training, follow these recommendations four times a week:

- **Week 7:** Walk two miles in thirty-eight minutes.

- **Week 8:** Walk two miles in thirty-six minutes.

- **Week 9:** Walk two miles in under thirty-five minutes.

Exercise Mistakes

The American Council on Exercise (ACE) asked three thousand of their certified fitness professionals nationwide to report the worst mistakes they see people making in the gym. "At best," reports ACE, "these mistakes may simply mean the difference between an effective and an ineffective workout; at worst, the mistakes can be costly, leading to strain and injury."

- **Not stretching enough.** You should warm up your muscles and then stretch them before and after aerobic activity to keep them flexible and less prone to straining or pulling. (Stretching cold muscles can lead to injury.)

- **Lifting too much weight.** Build up the weight you heft gradually so you don't injure yourself by going for too much resistance.

- **Not warming up before aerobic exercise.** Walking before running helps muscles adjust to the demands of aerobic activity.

- **Not cooling down after a workout.** Not taking time to lower your heart rate and stretch your muscles makes you less limber and can be dangerous.

- **Exercising too intensely.** Weekend warriors, who try to cram a week's worth of exercise into two days, are vulnerable to this mistake, which can lead to injury or burnout.

- **Not drinking enough water.** Even if you're not thirsty, it is important to drink sufficient amounts of water before and while exercising to replenish your body's fluids.

- **Leaning too heavily on the stairstepper,** so your weight is supported on the rails. This defeats the purpose of the exercise. Instead, step at a lower intensity—one at which you can maintain good posture while lightly resting your hands on the rails for balance.

- **Not exercising intensely enough.** If you're aiming for an aerobic workout, you want to work up at least a light sweat and get your heart rate into the training zone (above 60 percent of your maximum heart rate).

- **Jerking while lifting weights.** If you have to jerk a weight to lift it, you're lifting too much weight—and you're apt to strain your muscles.

- **Consuming energy bars and sports drinks during moderate workouts.** Unless you're working out for two hours or more per day, most fitness experts say you don't need an energy bar or drink in the middle of a workout to keep going.

The Right Equipment

Whether you're walking, running, golfing, or playing tennis, pay attention to your feet. Look for sneakers that are constructed to support your feet; oftentimes, sport-specific shoes are good choices. "Any tennis or walking shoe that costs $30 or more should be supportive for walking purposes," advises Susan Johnson, Ed.D., director of continuing education at the Cooper Institute for Aerobics Research (a division of the Cooper Aerobics Center) in Dallas, Texas. The sneakers should be comfortable and lightweight, with a well-cushioned rubber or crepe sole. You should have a half inch of space in the toebox, and the shoe should prevent your foot from rolling to either side while you're walking.

Also take advantage of new clothing technology, Johnson advises. Purchase workout garments with air holes in them for summer, and those made of synthetic fibers that pull moisture away from the body for winter.

Strength Training

As a natural course of events, most people lose muscle as they age—about a half pound of muscle a year starting after age twenty. That's of concern, because the less muscle you have, the more effort it takes to perform ordinary tasks—from climbing the stairs to lifting a grocery bag. In turn, the more energy it takes to do each little task, the more pooped it will make you feel.

Research indicates, however, that muscle loss isn't inevitable if you take steps to combat it. Oftentimes it's a result more of misuse and disuse of muscles than of nature's way. Recent ground-breaking research from Tufts University has even discovered that with strength training you can rebuild lost muscle mass after age fifty (that's something researchers thought couldn't happen). Strength training can also improve your strength, stamina, flexibility, balance, and coordination; preserve bone; and reduce your chance of injury.

Don't get yourself intimidated by the term "strength training." Yes, it can mean pumping handheld free weights or working out on weight machines. But it also means using rubber bands or tubing for resistance, or performing calisthenic exercises. All of these will tone and build muscle.

The American Council on Exercise (ACE) recommends doing twenty minutes of strength training at least twice a week—in addition to aerobic exercise. If you use weights, start at a low weight and progress slowly so you don't hurt yourself; you should be able to do three sets of twelve repetitions before you move on to a heavier weight. Don't hold your breath as you lift; instead breathe normally. Be sure to hit all the muscle groups and give yourself at least two days between workouts so your muscles get adequate rest. (You can, however, strength train on the same days as you work out aerobically; you can also alternate days.)

One of the best things about strength training: you'll probably notice an immediate improvement in your strength and muscle tone. And the more muscle you build, the more fat you'll burn—even while you're sleeping—which may help you lose weight. That's because muscle tissues consume calories faster than do fat tissues, boosting your metabolism.

STREET SMARTS

Alan, age forty-seven and a telecommunications consultant, says "I find that I get the biggest bang for my buck when I exercise early in the day: it boosts my metabolism and gives me a surge of energy. Exercising first thing also ensures that I won't skip a session because my day gets too busy."

A body-building champion, Alan lifts weights four to five days a week for an hour and a half. In winter, he also plays tennis or walks on the treadmill; in summer, he waterskis each morning before breakfast. "My wife, Jan, and I are out on the water at 7 A.M.," he says. "I find that so invigorating: the birds are singing, the lake water is clean and cool, and I feel fresh and rested. For me, waterskiing is a great way to power up for the day."

SMART SOURCES

American Council on
   Exercise (ACE)
5820 Oberlin Drive
San Diego, CA 92121-
   3787
800-825-3636
www.acefitness.org/
   fitfacts

Go to the "Fit Facts"
section on the Web
site, or call ACE for the
name of a local certi-
fied fitness instructor
or trainer.

Centers for Disease
   Control and
   Prevention
National Center for
   Chronic Disease
   Prevention and
   Health Promotion
Division of Nutrition
   and Physical Activity
MS K-46
4770 Buford Highway, NE
Atlanta, GA 30341
888-CDC-4NRG
(888-232-4674)
www.cdc.gov/nccdphp

Download "Physical
Activity and Health: A
Report of the Surgeon
General" from the Web
site.

Boost Your Energy—
and Your Mood

Many people intuitively get moving when they want to pump up their energy level, change their mood, or reduce tension. What they probably don't realize is that psychological research supports this self-help strategy: even a brisk ten-minute walk can immediately improve your mood, whereas regular exercise can confer an overall sense of mental well-being. And that's not all exercise is good for: it relieves stress, anxiety, and depression (perhaps even preventing these ailments), gives you creative oomph, enhances your self-esteem, and gives you a sense of mastery. It may even help you think more clearly.

Over the past couple of decades, more than one thousand scientific articles have been published investigating the psychological effects of exercise. Most have sought an answer to a basic question: "Does exercise make you feel better?" With a resounding "yes" now in hand, researchers are moving on to the second phase of research—trying to figure out how much of an effect activity has, and what types of exercise, intensity levels, and duration you need to achieve psychological benefits.

Though they cannot offer an individualized exercise prescription, exercise experts such as Thomas Plante, Ph.D., associate professor of psychology at Santa Clara University in California, can make some preliminary recommendations. For instance, it doesn't appear that exercise has to be aerobic to be psychologically beneficial. "A few studies indicate that it may not even be exercise itself or the physical fitness you gain from activity that produces beneficial effects, but rather the sense of self-mastery or the social support you derive from it," says Dr. Plante. It's most important that activity be continuous and rhythmic—walking, swimming, biking, and rowing are good—rather than intermittent. You should avoid activities that spark a competitive urge since they can actually provoke a bad mood.

As for duration, intensity, and frequency, most psychologists and exercise physiologists are sticking with the government recommendations for physical health as also being beneficial for the mind—thirty minutes of moderate-intensity activity most days of the week.

Add Relaxation and Meditation to Your Workout

"The best energy-building activities are those that have a meditative mind-body connection," says Michael Scholtz. "Activities such as yoga and tai chi, for instance, rest the mind and exercise the body; they also help get out the bad energy or chi, and let in the good energy." Furthermore, research indicates that when you perform yoga, the progressive contracting and releasing of various large muscle groups actually prompts the brain to release chemicals that make you feel relaxed yet alert.

"Almost any workout can become energy-building, if you put a mind aspect into it," continues Scholtz. For instance, you can add a meditative

SMART SOURCES

American College of
   Sports Medicine
P.O. Box 1440
Indianapolis, IN
   46202-1440
317-634-7817
www.acsm.org

Check out the "Public
Information Feature"
on the Web page.

The President's
   Council on Physical
   Fitness and Sports
Box SG
701 Pennsylvania
   Avenue, NW, Suite
   250
Washington, D.C.
   20004
202-272-3421

Request informational
materials, including a
quarterly newsletter
and the *PCPFS
Physical Activity and
Fitness Research
Digest*.

aspect to walking by forcing out all mental distractions and focusing in on a "mantra"—a word or series of words. Many people use the Transcendental Meditation word "om" as their mantra; "calm," "one," and "yes" are other good choices. Carolyn Scott Kortge, author of *The Spirited Walker: Fitness Walking for Clarity, Balance, and Spiritual Connection*, suggests using the phrases "right here, right now" or "I am here and I am walking." She describes the following technique: Do a gentle warm up and stretch and then pick up your walking pace. Observe good posture, but keep your eyes focused on the path. Silently, start to repeat your mantra over and over again in your head. If thoughts invade, go back to your mantra. Do this for ten to fifteen minutes. (Alternatively, you can focus your mind on counting the number of steps you take on your walk.)

Using meditative techniques while you're exercising gives your brain a much needed break from the stresses of the day. It also induces the "Relaxation Response," a calming of the body and mind that can have long-term health benefits (see chapter 6).

Eating for Energy

Although you don't want to eat a full meal within an hour of a workout because it can slow you down and produce discomfort, you do want something in your stomach to fuel your body. Oftentimes, a healthy protein-carbohydrate snack is the answer—fruit juice and a bagel, peanut butter with crackers, or yogurt with a piece of fruit are good choices.

If you're working out really hard and for longer than an hour, you might want to turn to energy bars or gels (Power Bar, Power Gel, Clif Bar) or drinks (Gatorade, Cytomax, Powerade) to give you a boost. These carbohydrate-rich products work by keeping your blood sugar up during exercise, sparing your muscle's glycogen stores for long-term use. The drinks also keep you hydrated and replace electrolytes (minerals such as potassium and sodium) that you sweat out during activity. (If you're working out for less than an hour, drink water instead—at least one cup for every fifteen minutes of activity.) All of the energy bars, gels, and drinks are easy to digest, so you get a quick energy bang from them. "Because they contain complex carbohydrates, you also get a more sustained boost than you would from a candy bar," notes Scholtz. Beware, though, you also get about 110 to 250 calories per serving.

The Perils of Too Much Exercise

The maxim "More is better" doesn't always apply to physical activity. Overexercising (or overtraining) can actually zap energy and rob your body of important nutrients, reports Kenneth Cooper, M.D., M.P.H., of the Cooper Aerobics Center. "I used to think that you could never exercise too much," he says. "But in 1982, it became clear that overexercising, such as running more than fifteen miles a week, conveyed no further cardiovascular benefit than running less. It also markedly increased the risk of muscle and joint injuries."

SMART MOVE

You don't have to join a gym or buy expensive equipment to get the exercise you need to boost your pep. In a survey of 410 people, psychologist Robert E. Thayer, Ph.D., found that walking is a favored antidote to flagging energy. "Walking for just ten minutes enhances energy for thirty minutes to two hours," he notes. It also wipes out a bad mood; reduces tension, nervousness, anxiety, fear, and other stress reactions; and helps people feel more optimistic.

Listening to music, socializing with others; performing household chores; engaging in hobbies, fun activities, or shopping; reading; and writing also rate high as strategies for lifting the spirit, reducing tension, and building pep in the long run.

Signs You're Overdoing It

Elite athletes aren't the only ones who fall prey to the effects of overtraining. The average gym-goer can suffer symptoms of this phenomenon, too. Here's how to tell if you're exercising too hard or too much:

Too Much Exercise

• Your resting heart rate goes up by 10 percent or more; for example, if it used to be 70 beats per minute (bpm) in the morning and it's now 77 bpm.

• You lose your appetite or experience stomach upsets or headaches.

• You're unusually moody, irritable, or depressed.

• You feel generally worn out and "stale."

• You experience lapses in concentration.

• It takes greater physical effort to perform an exercise you've been doing for a while.

• Your coordination declines.

• It takes you longer to bounce back from a workout session—aches and pains linger or you develop a chronic injury such as shin splints or tendonitis.

• You start to get sick frequently—for instance, you get a cold that won't go away.

• If you're a woman, you stop getting menstrual periods.

Remedy: Take a day or more off, pull back on intensity and duration of exercise, and try cross-training.

Too Little Exercise

• You feel sluggish.

• You gain weight.

• You experience stress symptoms such as muscle tension, headache, or lower-back pain.

Remedy: Pump up the volume and/or intensity of your workouts.

In the early 1990s, Dr. Cooper noticed that many of his patients who exercised excessively were developing cancer, cataracts, and heart disease. That was ironic; these people were supposed to be the most healthy of all. He theorized that the damage was due to increased amounts of what's known as free radicals—unstable oxygen molecules—being released into the body in response to exercise, exposure to environmental pollutants, and the regular process of metabolism. He and others further theorized that these damaged oxygen molecules harm healthy cells, precipitating illness.

Dr. Cooper believes that elite athletes can fend off some of this free radical damage by increasing their intake of antioxidant vitamins. He recommends 1,000 milligrams a day of vitamin C, 400 international units (IUs) of vitamin E (in its natural form, signified by d-alpha-tocopherol rather than dl-alpha-tocopherol on the label), and 25,000 IUs of beta carotene.

Sample Exercise Time Log

Activity	Time Spent
Parked the car ¼ mile from the mall	10 minutes
Weeded the garden	15 minutes
Walked the dog	5 minutes
TOTAL	30 minutes

Your Exercise Time Log

Activity	Time Spent
TOTAL	__ minutes

SMART SOURCES

To learn more about walking, check out these publications:

The Walking Handbook
Susan Johnson, Ed.D.
The Cooper Institute for Aerobics Research
800-635-7050

American College of Sports Medicine Fitness Book (second edition)
Available in bookstores

Walking Magazine
Customer Service Department
P.O. Box 5073
Harlan, IA 51593
800-829-5585

Building Exercise Into Your Life

The biggest challenge most people face when they think about exercise is finding the time or the motivation. The great thing about the new moderate exercise guidelines is that they encourage you to incorporate activity into your daily routine: climb stairs, for instance, instead of taking the elevator or escalator, or park far away from your office or the mall and walk rather than parking right next store. Ten minutes here and there is better than the never-achieved half hour you meant to spend at the gym.

Dr. James Rippe offers these tips for finding time to exercise:

• **Recognize your excuses about exercise as just that—excuses—and find ways around them.** "Be honest with yourself: you find time for things that really matter to you, so you can do the same with exercise," he advises. "Personally, I don't have time *not* to exercise."

If your excuse is that you don't like to exercise, for instance, delve deeper for the reason you feel that way. Say you find exercise boring. Well, you may not be doing something you enjoy. If you're running by yourself and you're really not a loner or a self-motivator, you're apt to quickly abandon that routine. It would be better for you to find a regular group to run with or a team sport to play instead. Conversely, if you're more of a loner who finds exercise a big yawn, try watching TV or listening to a book on tape while you walk on the treadmill.

Likewise, if you find exercise painful, tone down your routine. You're probably working out too hard or doing something wrong. The "go for the burn" mantra popularized by Jane Fonda is long dead. Exercise does not have to mean sweating, losing your breath, or pain.

• **Adopt an exercise-positive frame of mind.** Look at exercise as something to do for fun and look for activities that you already enjoy. Don't try just one thing, either; try a variety—swimming, tennis, running, water aerobics, yoga, boating, or whatever else strikes your fancy. Vary your routine to fight boredom, which will help you stick with exercise and get the greater benefits of cross-training.

• **Chose activities that are convenient and fit in well with your lifestyle and schedule.** Walking at a brisk pace is ideal for most people. As for timing, many people find they're more likely to exercise regularly if they do it in the morning. "In a survey of five hundred CEOs I did for my book *Fit for Success,* I found that executives are three times more likely than others to exercise regularly, and most prefer doing it in the morning before their day gets out of control," reports Dr. Rippe. "I myself like to work out in the afternoon, because it helps me get rid of the day's stress. The point is to plan your day—every day—looking for times you can exercise." Caution: Don't get active within three hours of bedtime; that can interfere with sleep.

• **Look for opportunities to add to your daily tally, throughout your day.** Mow the lawn, walk the dog, climb stairs, jump rope while watching TV, wash the car, vacuum: these moderately vigorous tasks can make up your thirty minutes a day before you

THE BOTTOM LINE

Exercise is a critical component of any energy-producing regimen. Minimal exercise guidelines released in the past few years by the U.S. Surgeon General and other organizations encourage all Americans to accumulate thirty minutes of moderate-intensity activity most, if not all, days of the week. Exercise can be broken up into ten- to fifteen-minute segments over the course of the day, and everyday activities such as walking the dog and climbing the stairs can count toward your daily quota. Mind-body exercises such as yoga and tai chi are particularly helpful for reducing stress and producing calm energy.

Intensive aerobic exercise and strength-training sessions will give you even more energy and stamina.

know it. Use the exercise log (see page 97) to track your activity, or buy a pedometer and shoot for up to ten thousand steps a day.

But Remember: Easy Does It at First

Many new exercisers start out gung-ho, with plans to exercise for an hour or more every day. Most abandon their plans within days because they find exercise boring or difficult to fit into their schedule, or they hurt themselves by exercising too hard.

If you've been sedentary, start exercise gradually and work up to thirty-minute or longer exercise sessions. Be sure to warm up and cool down after each session to lessen the risk of injury.

If you're a man over forty or a woman over fifty or have risk factors for heart or lung disease or a chronic disorder such as diabetes, consult your doctor and have a resting and stress cardiogram test before you start exercising vigorously. You may have health problems you don't know about that could put you at risk for a serious event during exercise. Certainly, if you have an existing health problem, you should talk to your doctor before embarking on an exercise program.

In chapter 6, look for more lifestyle strategies for increasing energy, including tips on improving your sleep, using relaxation techniques to calm your mind and rejuvenate your body, and cultivating hobbies and interests.

Lifestyle Strategies for Increasing Vitality

Besides creating time for regular exercise and improving your diet, there are several lifestyle changes you can make to increase your zip. Yes, we know that the last thing you want is another list of tasks to accomplish, but these sensible strategies—from getting more and better sleep to learning and practicing relaxation techniques—can make a huge difference for you. Even if you adopt only one or two strategies from this chapter, you'll boost your pep and increase your feeling of well-being.

Practice Good Sleep Habits

Sleep disorders are a primary energy zapper, and they affect some 40 million Americans. Almost everyone has trouble sleeping occasionally, so it's important to learn the best ways to enhance sleep—so you'll rest better, be less sleepy during the day, and have more energy.

Here are some time-tested tips for improving your sleep.

• **Keep a regular sleep-and-wake schedule,** and stick to it (even on weekends). This will train your brain to get drowsy, and conversely perk up, just when you want it to.

• **Avoid caffeinated and alcoholic drinks** in the late afternoon and evening. Caffeine can keep you awake, and alcohol, although it may initially help you to doze off, may disrupt your sleep later in the night. Also avoid nicotine at night; it can delay sleep or make you less likely to experience deep sleep.

• **Don't have a heavy meal before bedtime,** and go light on the spices and sugar. The digestive process can keep you up.

• **Have a glass of warm low-fat milk** or a banana before bed. They both contain the amino acid tryptophan, which can make you sleepy.

• **Unwind for half an hour before bed.** Read, listen to calming music, or try a relaxation technique to prepare you for sleep. Try to rid yourself of anxious thoughts.

• **Exercise on a regular basis,** but not within three hours of bedtime. Your body is aroused after a workout and needs a chance to relax and get ready for sleep.

• **Take a hot bath** three hours before bedtime. The hot water will raise your body temperature. The interceding hours will lower it, priming you for sleep.

• **Create an inviting sleep environment**—one free of noise, light, and distractions. Make sure you have sufficient curtains on the windows to block out light and use a white-noise or nature-sounds machine to mask irritating street noise. The room should be between 60° to 75°F (a cooler temperature promotes sleep), the mattress and pillow should be firm and comfortable.

• **If you're tossing and turning thirty minutes after going to bed, don't just lie there wishing for sleep.** This will only create an association between the bed and sleeplessness. Instead, get up and engage yourself in a relaxing task—reading a book (nothing too stimulating) or listening to soothing music. Try not to get riled up or into worrisome thinking patterns. Continue the calming activity until you feel sleepy, then climb into bed and try again.

• **Use your bed only for sleep and sex.** Don't watch TV, read, or work there.

• **If you're having trouble sleeping at night, avoid naps during the day.** And certainly avoid naps that are longer than half an hour.

• **Have a cup of valerian or chamomile tea** before bed. Both herbs are mild natural sedatives.

• **Scent your pillow** with a drop of pure lavender oil. It may help induce sleep.

• **Look over the medications that you are taking—** prescription and over-the-counter—for warnings that they may cause insomnia. Talk to your doctor or pharmacist about using different drugs that won't impair your ability to rest.

• **Take over-the-counter sleep aids cautiously.** A 1993 Gallup survey of three hundred sleep experts indicates that only 1 percent consider these products to be "very effective." They can also cause side effects, such as daytime sleepiness.

Take Frequent Work Breaks

Americans now live in a twenty-four-hour, seven-day-a-week society. Many of us work fifty or more hours a week, and take our work home with us. "The U.S. business world's mentality tends to be, the more hours worked, the more work produced," writes energy expert Ann McGee-Cooper in her book *You Don't Have to Go Home from Work Exhausted!* "This idea applies not only to the stretch of hours worked on a given day and week, but also to the minimal amount of personal break time allotted to each day."

McGee-Cooper says that research now shows that we typically hit a productivity high point at a certain time of day; efficiency, accuracy, motivation, creativity are all downhill from there. Hence, working longer doesn't necessarily equate with being more productive. Studies also indicate that most people can only operate at a peak comprehension and processing level for sixty minutes at a time.

McGee-Cooper says that the best way to maintain energy and productivity throughout the workday is to replenish energy stores before they are scraping the bottom of the barrel. Here's how:

• **Get up from your desk every fifteen to thirty minutes** to stretch and walk around. This will reduce physical and mental tension, and fatigue. (Concentrating intently on a mental task can be energy draining, and sitting for hours on end signals your brain to start shutting down for sleep.)

• **Try to schedule two short work breaks in the morning and the afternoon.** "In general," says

Making a Living—and a Difference

You'd like a job that makes you feel good about yourself and about going to work, right? That's the best way to an energized lifestyle.

Well, you're not alone in this desire: according to a Roper poll, 86 percent of working adults yearn for a job that helps make the world a better place— and gives them personal satisfaction in the process. As long as the pay is adequate, they'd prefer that to making a lot of money.

"Having a job you're committed to because you feel it's worthwhile is a great morale booster: you have a real sense of pride, purpose, and self-value," notes Constance Buxer, Ph.D., a New York City psychoanalyst and career counselor. "Both the psychological literature and my experience with patients show that improved morale leads to less absenteeism and lateness, greater productivity, and less physical and mental illness," she says.

McGee-Cooper, "it's time to take a break whenever you feel a lack of motivation, feel tense, start procrastinating, are engaging in complex work or work that requires a high level of concentration, or when you hit a mental block." Make sure whatever you do during your energy break is very different from what you were just doing. For instance, if you just had a tense meeting with a coworker, go into your office and read a fun magazine for a few minutes to decompress. "Or use your breaks as a reward for accomplishing difficult or bothersome tasks," she suggests.

• **Meditate at your desk** once or twice a day.

• **Take a walk** at midday or go to the gym to rev yourself up for the afternoon.

• **Listen to energizing music** while you're working. Mozart is particularly good. (See page 125.)

• **Take a mental health day** every once in a while (call it a sick day if you must). Then indulge yourself for the day without guilt.

• **Investigate flextime options** with your employer, and the opportunity to work from home a few days a week. This will cut down on your commute and work interruptions. (Most work-at-homers will tell you they get far more done in a shorter amount of time at home than at the office, largely because they're not interrupted as often.)

Take Frequent Vacations

Europeans have recognized the value of extended and frequent vacations for ages; they take several weeks off each year, and in some cases the breaks are mandatory. In contrast, Americans are lucky if they can steal away for a long weekend. (Three- and four-day weekends are terrific, but you also need longer periods of time—at least a week—away from the world to forget your cares and really unwind.)

Other good tips to keep in mind:

• **Take vacations from your kids.** Even the most devoted parent needs an occasional respite from kids' demands and needs. Schedule weekends or vacations with other adults, and leave the kids and the work at home.

• **Disconnect.** Don't bring pagers, laptop computers, or other electronic equipment connecting you to the office on vacation. A vacation is meant to be a break from work—not an office away from the office.

Turn Off the World As Often As Possible

"In today's society, we're constantly bombarded with information—from TV, newspapers, magazines, and the Internet. Most of this information shows us the worst of life, makes us feel bad, and casts the world as a scary place," says Thomas Plante, Ph.D., a psychologist at Santa Clara University in California. The information flow also puts us on overload, since all those facts and figures coming at us need to be processed somehow.

Here are some suggestions for turning off the world:

• **Decrease the amount of time you spend watching TV** (especially the news), or stop watching it altogether. Also lighten up on reading newspapers and news magazines.

• **Prioritize** the things you give your attention to. Think about your goals and desires in life, and drop the activities that sap your energy and don't fulfill you. In a word: simplify.

• **Try to stop multitasking**—doing several things at once to save time. It's stressful and, because you're distracted, it doesn't really improve your efficiency that much. Instead, focus on one thing at a time; once you've finished one task, start another and make your way down the list of "to dos." Doing single tasks will make you feel much calmer and in control.

• **Banish guilt** about not doing as much as you think you should, or about enjoying a break when you think you should be working. Guilt is a largely useless emotion that drains mental vitality.

• **Pay attention to body signals.** Chronic headaches, muscle tension, back pain, colds, and flus all point to stress. They're a message from your body to back off and relax. Reducing stress can bring your immunity back up to par and may rid you of many of these symptoms.

• **Organize** your time, your life, your house, and your desk to maximize things you like to do and minimize things you don't.

• **Decrease clutter.** When you live in clutter, you can't find what you need and you unnecessarily waste precious energy.

Learn to Live Constructively

You'd love to embark on an energy-boosting plan, but you have a million excuses to stop you from getting started: you're too tired right now, you need to start dinner, you have a phone call to make . . . your momentary feelings beat out your best intentions every time.

Enter Constructive Living, a philosophy/action therapy that says: Forget about your feelings and

SMART SOURCES

To learn more about Constructive Living, contact the ToDo Institute at:

P.O. Box 874
Middlebury, VT 05753
800-950-6034
www.anamorph.com/
    todo/

They have an online library of articles, a bookstore, and information about a long-distance learning program.

You can also pick up Constructive Living techniques by reading books by David Reynolds, Ph.D., the man who melded Eastern with Western ideas to create this "Just Do It" philosophy of life. He's written some twenty titles on the topic, including *Rainbow Rising from a Stream, Thirsty, Swimming in the Lake,* and *Even in Summer the Ice Doesn't Melt.*

your excuses. Just get out there and do something, anything, that takes you one step closer to your goal.

Constructive Living is a westernized version of Japanese Morita philosophy, which regards emotions to be as natural, fleeting, and uncontrollable as the weather. It acknowledges that you can't beat your feelings into submission or avoid having them just by sheer strength of will. So instead of fighting them, Constructive Living tells you to notice the emotions you're experiencing and accept them. Then, focus on things you can change—namely, your behavior. Say, for instance, that you don't feel like getting up one morning for a job interview— even though it may change your life for the better. Constructive Living tells you to tip your hat to how you feel but still do what needs to be done: get up, take a shower, get dressed, and go. Chances are you'll start to feel more upbeat as you get ready.

Gregg Krech, a Constructive Living instructor who runs the ToDo Institute in Middlebury, Vermont, explains that "We've traditionally been taught that we have to fix our feelings before we can take action. But actual life experience shows it works mostly the other way around: we change our feelings by doing."

If you'd like to try this practical, commonsensical, and easy-to-understand therapy, get started by keeping a diary of your feelings and actions to see how the former may be inhibiting the latter. On the left hand of each page, make a narrow column to record the time, and on the right make two wide columns, one to record feelings, one to record actions. Throughout the day, make note of your feelings and actions in various situations. According to Constructive Living experts, this technique will help you to see that you can accomplish what you need to do *in spite of your emotional state.*

Another way to start living more constructively is to set very small goals, focusing on what needs to be done right now. Going back to the job scenario, if you've been laid off, you can't just sit around and sulk, hoping another position will fall into your lap. You've got to set a goal—in this case, maybe looking through newspaper ads and making five phone calls a day.

Ultimately, the value of concentrating on small goals is that confidence follows success. Step-by-step achievement with a series of small goals can propel you to be more adventurous and will make you more resilient.

Lose Weight

There's a direct connection between your weight and your energy level: the more pounds you have to tote around, the more energy it saps from you.

Here are the basic tenets of any safe, healthy weight-loss plan:

• **Eat no fewer than 1,200 calories a day.** Less than that, and your body, convinced that it's facing possible starvation, will resist weight-loss efforts and start to hang on to fat. You'll feel tired to boot.

• **Follow the Food Guide Pyramid** and eat a balanced diet with an emphasis on fruits, vegetables, and grains. Keep your fat intake to less than 30 percent of your daily calories. (See chapter 4 for more information.)

• **Learn about proper portion sizes.** (Again, see chapter 4 for more information.)

SMART SOURCES

Thin for Life: 10 Keys to Success from People Who Have Lost Weight and Kept It Off
Anne M. Fletcher, M.S., R.D.

Eating Thin for Life: Food Secrets and Recipes from People Who Have Lost Weight and Kept It Off
Anne M. Fletcher, M.S., R.D.

Weight Watchers International
Consumer Affairs Department
175 Crossways Park West
Woodbury, NY 11797-2055
800-651-6000

Ask for local meeting times, locations, and information about joining.

• **Count calories and fat grams.** Buy books that list calorie and fat counts for many foods and use them to calculate your daily intakes. Also, become a label reader.

• **Shoot to lose one to two pounds a week.** Although you may lose several pounds a week at the start of a diet or if you're very heavy, once you settle into your program your target should be modest but continuous weight loss. More than one to two pounds a week, and you'll be dieting too fanatically, putting your health and your willpower at risk.

• **Exercise frequently**—preferably every day. Studies show that following a routine exercise program is the number one predictor of whether someone will keep weight off once he or she has lost it. (See chapter 5 for suggestions on how to incorporate more physical activity into your life.)

• **Keep a food plan and a diary**—and write down every crumb and morsel you consume. You'll probably be amazed at how much you're eating. Research suggests that overweight people tend to underestimate their caloric intake by one-third if they don't record what they eat. They also tend to overestimate their exercise level by one-half.

• **Eat slowly.** It takes twenty minutes after you've started eating for your brain to get the message that you're full.

• **Think about how you'll handle stressful emotional and social situations** and deal with lapses so they don't sink your weight-loss efforts. For example, if you're due to attend a party, you might plan to have a cup of low-fat soup or some fruit to fill you up before you go. Or you might bring a low-calorie dish with you to the gathering.

• **Don't deprive yourself of foods you love.** This will only set you up for a binge or lapse. Instead, indulge in these foods in moderation—a slice of pizza or an ice cream cone once a week, or a small piece of chocolate every other day. Work the calories into your daily meal plan and cut back on other foods when you eat them.

• **Plan and prepare your meals** in advance so you won't be tempted to eat fatty foods on the fly.

• **Choose a realistic weight goal.** You might have a hankering to be model-thin—but your body type will likely make that impossible. Instead, shoot for a goal that is realistic for you. Even a 10 percent overall weight loss can have a significant and beneficial effect on your health and energy reserves.

• **Lose weight your way.** There are many options available to overweight people today: Weight Watchers, Take Off Pounds Sensibly (TOPS), Jenny Craig, and Overeaters Anonymous, to name but a few. One or more of these options may be just what you need, or you may be better off devising your own plan, one that suits your personality, lifestyle, and eating needs.

Consume Alcohol Wisely

Alcohol is problematic for a number of reasons: It can add pounds, impair sleep, sap B vitamins and amino acids from the body, and dehydrate you. It also depresses the central nervous system and acts as a sedative (although initially you may perk up, alcohol ultimately lets you back down). Most experts see no harm in occasionally imbibing—there's even a bank of research that shows that moderate alcohol intake is good for your health. But excessive consumption—over one drink a day for women and two drinks for men—is not advised.

Follow these tips for avoiding a hangover, if you do indulge:

• **Drink slowly and on a full stomach** so the liquor will enter your bloodstream more slowly. You might want to drink fruit juice with alcohol, too; the sugar in fruit assists the body in burning alcohol so it leaves your bloodstream faster.

• **Have a couple of glasses of water before you go to bed** to counter alcohol's dehydrating effects and replenish your body's fluids.

• **Do not take pain relievers when you have been drinking.** Not only will aspirin and ibuprofen irritate your stomach (as will liquor), but acetaminophen (Tylenol) has been found to cause liver damage when used in conjunction with alcohol.

Stop Smoking

How does your energy level relate to smoking? It impairs your breathing, which can cut into your athletic performance and predispose you to lung disease. Of course, smoking also does a number on your health: medical experts say it's the single most preventable risk factor for disease and death.

Quitting smoking quickly restores the body to nonsmoking condition. You'll find it easier to breathe, you'll cough less, you'll have more energy and stamina, and you'll feel better physically and emotionally (the latter because you've done something so good for yourself and so tough to do). The trick is to quit, and quit for good.

There are now several aids to help you do just that. All address the addictive nature of nicotine and help quell cigarette cravings and withdrawal symptoms.

Over-the-counter products include:

• Nicotine gum (Nicorette)

• Nicotine patches (Nicotrol and NicoDerm CQ)

Prescription products include:

• Nicotine patches (Habitrol and Prostep)

• Nicotine nasal spray (Nicotrol NS)

• A nicotine inhaler (Nicotrol Inhaler)

• An oral medication (Zyban)

SMART SOURCES

American Lung Association
1740 Broadway
New York, NY 10019-4374
800-LUNG-USA
(800-586-4872)
www.lungusa.org

Ask for the free *Quit Smoking Action Plan.*

American Cancer Society
1599 Clifton Road, NE
Atlanta, GA 30329
800-ACS-2345
www.cancer.org

Request *Commit to Quit, Smart Move,* and other brochures, and get a number for a local support group.

Agency for Health Care Policy and Research
Publications Clearinghouse
P.O. Box 8547
Silver Spring, MD 20907
800-358-9295
www.ahcpr.gov/

Request *You Can Quit Smoking* (Consumer Version, Clinical Practice Guideline Number 18).

Research shows that by combining nicotine replacement products with behavioral modification you can double quit rates. So can the use of Zyban.

Practice Relaxation Techniques

It's paradoxical, but one of the best ways to boost energy is to practice relaxation techniques. These exercises offer a time-out or respite from the world. They stop the chaos cluttering your mind, and the constant deluge of thoughts and feelings. They rejuvenate you in a way similar to sleep (although the brain-wave patterns produced by these exercises are different from those generated during sleep). They create a sense of peace and calm, and restore energy reserves so that you can approach daily tasks and problems with a stronger, less tense, and more balanced state of mind.

Any number of relaxation techniques can do the trick. You can start with simple deep breathing or the Relaxation Response, and progress to more complicated techniques like tai chi. On the following pages, you'll find descriptions of some common relaxation exercises; try one, try them all. But try to adopt at least one and do it on a regular, if not daily, basis.

Deep Breathing

Although breathing is a natural act—in fact, an unconscious act that is critical to our survival—most of us shortchange ourselves by breathing in a shallow manner. By making a conscious effort to breathe fully and draw oxygen deep into your lungs, experts say you can reduce fatigue and stress, and elicit relaxation and calm.

Try this technique for improving your breathing. Do it a couple of times a day for a couple of minutes at a time. Also call on it whenever you feel tense:

1. Lie down on your back or sit in a chair, whichever you prefer. Keep your back straight and your body loose.

2. Relax your stomach muscles.

3. Slowly and deeply inhale through your nose—enough to make your stomach round out. Hold the breath for a count of three. (When your belly puffs out with the inhalation of air, it means you are using your diaphragm and getting the oxygen deep into your lungs. Many of us don't fully expand our lungs; we tense our stomach muscles and breathe so shallowly that the air never makes it beyond the upper chest. If you're pushing your chest out and not your stomach when you inhale, you're not breathing deeply.)

4. Slowly exhale through your nose or mouth, pulling in your stomach muscles and gently pushing out the breath.

5. Repeat several times.

SMART MOVE

One of the best ways to boost your vitality is to volunteer your time. Research by Allan Luks, executive director of Big Brothers/Big Sisters of New York, reveals that those who perform charitable acts experience a helper's high—a surge in energy and good feelings about themselves and the world. Volunteers also experience improved health.

The key to getting the energy-boosting benefits of volunteering: the work you do must be on-site, hands-on, and connected to others. Writing a check won't give you the same lift as reading to the blind, hammering some nails for Habitat for Humanity, or mentoring a youngster.

Meditation

When you hear the word *meditation,* you likely think of Transcendental Meditation, or TM. This is the best known form of meditation, but there are numerous other techniques that have been around for centuries, such as Zen and yoga. All are designed to reduce stress, increase inner peace, and raise conscious awareness.

Harold H. Bloomfield, M.D., a devout TM practitioner since 1959 who studied with Maharishi Mahesh Yogi (the founder of TM) and the lead author of the book *TM: Discovering Inner Energy and Overcoming Stress,* suggests that if you're really interested in learning TM, you should study with someone officially trained in the technique.

To get you started, however, here are basic instructions:

1. Choose a quiet room. Sit cross-legged on the floor. Place your hands, palms upward and index fingers and thumbs touching, on your knees. Close your eyes.

2. Focus your attention on a word (also called a mantra). *Om* is the word typically associated with TM; in Sanskrit, it means "the word." Repeat your mantra silently to yourself.

3. When thoughts come to mind, gently push them away by refocusing on the word you have selected. Assume a passive attitude toward these intruding thoughts and your ability to perform the exercise. Instead of worrying about doing the technique correctly, just do it without judging yourself.

4. Continue the exercise for fifteen to twenty minutes. Perform it daily—and ideally twice a day, at whatever time your schedule allows.

The Relaxation Response

Herbert Benson, M.D., of Harvard University, coined the term *Relaxation Response* in the 1970s to describe an exercise he developed that draws on techniques of meditation and deep breathing, and incorporates muscle relaxation into the mix. Performed once or twice a day, Dr. Benson says that the Relaxation Response will help to reduce fatigue and stress, slow your breathing and heart rate, improve your sleep, and conserve your energy.

Here's the technique:

1. Find a quiet room and sit in a comfortable, relaxed position. Many people like to sit cross-legged on the floor or in a chair. Lying down isn't advised, as you may fall asleep.

2. Close your eyes.

3. Start to deeply relax your muscles, starting with your feet and slowly moving up to your face, one part of the body at a time (first your toes, then your heels, your ankles, your calves, your shins, etc.).

4. Breathe through your nose and take notice of your breathing. Keep your breathing natural and rhythmic.

5. As you exhale, say the word *one* to yourself.

6. If you experience any distracting thoughts—and you will—push them away and refocus on your word or sound. Stop yourself from worrying about how well you're performing the exercise; this can lead to a less then optimal result.

7. Continue this for ten to twenty minutes.

Visualization

This relaxation technique is often used to enhance physical and work performance and to relieve pain. It incorporates relaxation techniques with positive self-talk in the form of images. Visualization can prime you to perform better and can be used as an imaginative form of rehearsal.

Here's how it works:

1. Start by performing deep breathing (or the Relaxation Response).

2. Conjure up a pleasant scene in your mind—a day at the beach, the woods, the mountains—anything that makes you feel good and peaceful. Use all of your senses to put yourself into that place. Feel the warm sunshine on your face, hear the sound of the waves crashing onto the beach, smell the salty ocean air.

3. Alternatively, after you relax, try to experience a situation that you're anxious about—and recast it in your mind in a positive way. (This is called guided imagery.) For instance, visualize yourself running in a race—and winning it. Or imagine yourself making a presentation to a big client, and having the client immediately offer you the project. Don't rush through the process—take it step by step, from when you greet the client at the door, escort him to the conference room, offer him coffee, turn down the lights, hit the button on your laptop to bring up your presentation graphics, and onward to the successful conclusion.

Yoga, Tai Chi, and Massage

Other forms of relaxation techniques are making their way into the mainstream's consciousness. They include:

Yoga

Yoga, much like meditation, has been reborn in the 1990s. Six million people have adopted this five-thousand-year-old system of exercise and rejuvination—including singer Madonna—and one in ten Americans say they'd like to try it, according to a *Yoga Journal* poll.

Yoga is an active yet quiet form of meditation and deep breathing designed to relax and clear the mind, combined with a series of poses designed to slowly and gently stretch the muscles. The goal of yoga is to balance the body and mind.

Hatha yoga is the predominant form of yoga practiced in the United States. However, as with other relaxation techniques, numerous variations have sprung into being, some more physically challenging than others.

Yoga requires patience and attention to your body. Stretching poses are held for several seconds

SMART SOURCES

Videos
Yoga

Introductory

Yoga Journal's Yoga for Beginners

Kathy Smith's New Yoga Basics

Intermediate

Yoga Journal's Yoga Practice for Energy

Ali MacGraw's Yoga Mind and Body

Tai Chi

David Carradine's Chi Kung

Tai Chi with David Dorian Ross

SMART SOURCES

*The Complete Book of
   Tai Chi*
Stewart McFarlane

Yoga for Stress Relief
Swami Shivapre-
   mananda

at a time, and you are taught to breathe deeply while performing them. This is thought to boost blood and oxygen flow throughout the body, relieve stress, and increase energy.

Tai Chi

Tai chi is another form of active meditation. It is often referred to as a martial art, and enhances strength, flexibility, coordination, and balance—and boosts energy. Like other forms of meditation, it is also believed to stimulate the proper flow of chi (life energy) through the body. It was developed in China some five thousand years ago.

A tai chi practitioner performs a series of postures in a set sequence; the forms flow into one another as if the person were dancing. The goal is to almost "swim through the air." Many people like to perform tai chi outside—in movies you often see people doing the exercises on a beach—and in groups.

Massage

Massage may seem like a pure indulgence, but it has proven relaxation (and health) benefits. Many people report that they have greater energy when they get regular massages, and athletes rely on it for less-sore muscles. In fact, massage in its many varieties is designed to restore the body to its natural and optimal state of balance, reduce muscle tension, and increase blood circulation. Shiatsu massage, an Oriental form, was created to restore the free flow of chi through the body.

Use Music to Gain Energy

Most of us listen to music on a regular basis. Typically, we tune in for the joy of the experience. But there's more to music than sheer pleasure: research now shows it has a potent—almost magical—impact on the mind, body, and spirit. Music can even be used to improve your health.

"I am living proof of the power of music," says Don Campbell, author of *The Mozart Effect*, and the founder of the Institute for Music, Health and Education in Boulder, Colorado. "Four years ago, I was diagnosed with a life-threatening blood clot in my brain. I had two options: I could have major surgery to remove a third of my skull to prevent a stroke, or I could wait to see if the blood clot would dissolve spontaneously. I chose the latter option—largely because I believed I could use music to help my body heal itself.

"I began an intensive regimen of listening to classical and sacred music, humming, and visualization. Three weeks later, my clot had shrunk an inch and a half. The greatest danger of stroke had passed. Even my doctors were amazed and grudgingly admitted music may have played a role in my recovery."

Campbell says that he's not alone in having experienced the remarkable healing power of music on the ailing mind and body. There are now hundreds of scientific studies that validate its effects in reducing blood pressure, decreasing the need for painkillers after surgery, and relieving headaches.

Music can even boost productivity and alert-

STREET SMARTS

Marc, forty-two, a writer and editor, is hooked on music as an energy enhancer. "I always listen to jazz while I'm working because it sets a pace for me," he explains. "Lively, melodic music also helps me concentrate and block out the world, especially on days when I have a lot to accomplish. The rhythm energizes me; it gives me a creative charge and makes me set a fast pace and stick to the job for extended periods of time."

One caveat: Marc finds that only instrumentals are energy boosting during work hours. "Vocals draw my attention away from the manuscript I'm working on to the lyrics of the song. Instrumentals enhance my creative spirit and allow me to develop a highly focused sense of flow."

ness: A University of California study found that students who listened to ten minutes of Mozart before taking an SAT exam scored higher than did those who didn't listen to music. And in a University of Washington study, workers who listened to light classical music for ninety minutes while preparing a manuscript improved their accuracy rate by 21 percent.

Why Music Is Energizing

Music is amazing because it affects the body and the brain in three ways simultaneously, according to Campbell:

• **The rhythms change your heartbeat**—the heart rate tends to mimic the pace of the song, speeding up or slowing down in synch. Music rhythms can also change brain waves and breathing patterns. And some music, such as disco, induces a strong urge to move your body. Campbell calls music a "natural pacemaker."

• **The harmonies impact your feelings.** They can help you to let go of painful or angry emotions and to relish happy feelings. It's even been found that joyful, rich music, such as movie soundtracks, religious music, and marching band music, can boost the brain's production of natural painkillers (known as endorphins). Conversely, relaxing music can reduce the production of stress hormones.

• **The melodies stay in your head like language.** And if music has lyrics, those words take on a specific meaning that can affect your mood.

In addition to hearing music through your auditory system, you actually feel music vibrations on your skin and in your bones, Campbell says. These vibrating sounds have effects on your mood and many body functions, such as blood pressure, pulse, and temperature.

Why Mozart's Music Is Particularly Energizing

"Mozart's music is characterized by a very organized structure; the rhythms, melodies, and high frequencies he used have been shown to stimulate and charge the creative and motivational regions of the brain," says Campbell.

Several studies, many performed by the French physician Alfred Tomatis, M.D., indicate that listening to Mozart's compositions has a calming effect. His music has also been noted to increase spatial perception and to improve the ability to communicate feelings, concepts, and thoughts.

But you don't have to listen to Mozart or even to classical music to get a musical boost. "All forms of music can be used to create various effects," says Campbell.

He suggests the following musical selections for energizing the mind and body:

• **To perk up your mind:** Choose music, such as Mozart's violin concertos, that is in a high key and has a quick beat. The fast pace will hasten your heartbeat and breathing, increasing oxygen and blood flow to your brain and improving alertness and thinking capacity.

• **To energize your body:** Use dance music—look for pieces that have a lively beat and rhythm that force you to get moving. Disco, salsa, rhumba, country, or hip-hop can all work.

• **To improve mental stamina and concentration:** Play light, easy-paced music by Vivaldi, Mozart, Bach, or Handel while you work or study.

• **To improve physical stamina:** Listen to fast-paced, repetitive compositions—but avoid heavy rock music; studies show it can actually decrease athletic performance.

• **To unleash your creativity:** Select romantic, jazz, or New Age music; compositions by Debussy, Faure, and Ravel are all good choices.

• **To calm your mind:** Listen to Wagner's compositions or other music with a slow tempo and long, low sounds. This type of music will release physical tension and slow your breathing and thus your mind.

"Of course, the effects of music are most potent if you devote yourself to listening to it, and block out distractions," Campbell says. Choose a quiet, dark room and a comfortable chair, and close your eyes so you can hear better (your sense of hearing is more acute when your eyes are shut).

Set Free Your Right Brain, and Play Like a Child

When you're lacking in energy, it's often because you've lost the unstructured, childlike capacity for play, laughter, and joy. "So many people think of leisure time as a luxury rather than a necessity," says Ann McGee-Cooper, "but without play your life becomes out of balance."

Even when you think you're engaging in leisure-time activities, you may be conducting yourself in a far-too-adult and uptight way. For instance, in sports: Do you approach a game in a light-hearted way, like a child would? Or do you set out to compete at a certain level, beat your opponent, and boost your ego? The latter are left-brained approaches that can contribute to stress. (See chapter 2 to assess your brain dominance profile.) Real right-brained play releases tension, stimulates creativity, and causes the body to pump out endorphins (natural feel-good chemicals).

Some of the keys to the childlike, right-brained, free flow of energy include:

• **Being receptive to change.**

• **Being open to learning new things** and to being an awkward or imperfect beginner.

• **Experimenting** with a variety of approaches.

• **Jumping from one activity to another** as the mood strikes you.

WHAT MATTERS, WHAT DOESN'T

What Matters

• Finding strategies that work for you— rather than those that supposedly work for everyone.

• Simplifying your life as much as you can.

• Organizing your time better.

• Giving yourself a break—every day, every weekend, every year.

• Finding things that you love to do—that induce "flow."

What Doesn't

• Spending more time working.

• Catching up on sleep on the weekends rather than addressing a chronic sleep deficit.

•Addressing stress only on weekends, rather than every day.

• **Developing hobbies and avocations that are fun** and that give you a sense of purpose and meaning.

"Most of the high-energy behavior characteristic of kids can be used by adults to increase their energy as well," McGee-Cooper writes in her book *You Don't Have to Go Home from Work Exhausted!* "In fact, research indicates that most geniuses and top performers have retained these characteristics throughout adulthood."

McGee-Cooper also notes that high-energy people have learned how to integrate the left and right sides of the brain so they work together. These people fight brain duality, the scenario in which the characteristics of one side of the brain are considered superior to those of the other, and energy is wasted trying to suppress the attributes of the less-favored side. Instead, high-energy people appreciate, use, and value both sides of the brain.

Make Change Work for You

Change is a constant in our lives. We marry, have kids, switch jobs, move, make new friends, and learn new skills. Change is good because it is stimulating (there's nothing like a rut to sap your vitality). But change can also be scary.

"Trying to stop change is like trying to stop the seasons. You can't, because it's a higher force of nature," says Dennis O'Grady, Psy.D. A psychologist practicing in Dayton, Ohio, Dr. O'Grady has written a book called *Taking the Fear Out of Changing* based on what's he's learned from counseling more than one thousand clients in making effective changes.

Rather than merely reacting to changes that are forced upon you, Dr. O'Grady says you can learn how to create changes that will work for you. You can become a "change expert," embracing change rather than fearing it.

Try these strategies:

• **Look at change as a trusted ally** and not as the enemy. Study change. Look back on examples from your life where you chose to or were forced to change. How did you get through the change? What were the stages you went through? How did things turn out? You survived, right? Perhaps you even thrived. This sort of reflection can give you the confidence to make new changes.

• **Don't panic** when you feel afraid of positive changes, such as a new baby or a new job. "Fear is a normal part of changing," says Dr. O'Grady.

• **Take rejections and setbacks in stride.** Expect them and don't let them stop you from changing and doing what you really want to do.

• **Expect unexpected pain with every change you make.** "A change may not turn out the way you wanted it to," he says, "but if you keep with it, and keep changing, you'll get to a stage where there will also be joy, satisfaction, and success."

"Change means gain and loss," says Dr. O'Grady. "For instance, you can't live in two places at once or be both a stay-at-home mom and a full-time employee. But change also equals success. Whereas not changing—not going for what you really want

F.Y.I.

While some worry is okay for you—psychologists say it can actually prepare you to deal with bad situations—too much is stressful, unproductive, and energy-draining.

The trick to worrying less? Give yourself permission to worry. Studies have found this technique useful: Schedule a half hour's worth of worry time daily. During those thirty minutes, worry all you want, but try to be realistic. Don't catastrophize—turning a summer rainstorm into a certain car crash, for instance. At the end of the session, stop your worrisome thoughts. If you catch yourself worrying at other times of the day, quickly focus on something else.

in life—can build up resentments, regrets, and other negative emotions."

Find Flow

Mihaly Csikszentmihalyi, Ph.D., author of *Flow: The Psychology of Optimal Experience* and *Finding Flow*, has studied some three thousand people over three decades to find out how they have developed a peak sort of energy level that he calls *flow*. Flow, he writes, "is the state in which people are so involved in an activity that nothing else seems to matter; the experience itself is so enjoyable that people will do it even at great cost, for the sheer sake of doing it."

Flow can be achieved by people from all walks of life, of all genders, ages, and intellectual levels. It doesn't tend to come, however, unless you engage in an activity that challenges you and that you love. Passively watching television doesn't bring flow—and may sap pep and induce boredom—but weaving a rug or piecing a quilt together can elicit it. So can working on a crossword puzzle, playing chess, reading, listening to music, dancing, sailing, or crafting a bookcase, if that's what you love to do. Flow is a state of intense but effortless and enjoyable concentration—the type of situation where you look at the clock and are surprised to see that two hours have gone by in what seems like ten minutes.

To find out what will bring flow to your life, identify activities that you enjoy and pursue them, Dr. Csikszentmihalyi advises. This can be an intellectual or creative pursuit, a sport, or an art form. Then set challenging goals for yourself in relation to these activities; make the goals hard enough that you'll have to work toward them, but not so hard that they're impossible to achieve. "To create flow, the activity should lead to the growth of the self in some way," he says; "otherwise, you'll experience boredom and stagnation." You must be continually pushing yourself to scale a new level of achievement or performance.

Touch Others— and Be Touched

There's nothing like a good hug or the weight of a hand on your shoulder to make you feel better when you're down—and psychological research is now showing how very much we need to touch and be touched. Some fifty psychological studies have found that physical contact lowers anxiety, relieves depression, boosts alertness and mood, and reduces levels of stress hormones that can destroy the immune system, says Tiffany M. Field, Ph.D., founder and director of the Touch Research Institute at the University of Miami School of Medicine, where the studies were performed.

Despite these scientifically established benefits, American adults don't touch one another much. A landmark study of the behavior of couples at cafés found that the French touched over one hundred times during a thirty-minute period whereas Americans touched only once. "We're so afraid of being accused of abuse or harassment today that we're touch deprived," she says.

So how can you put more touch in your life? Dr. Field suggests you:

• **Make an effort to touch family members and friends more often**—hold hands, give backrubs, link arms, and kiss hello.

• **Pet a dog or cat**. There's excellent data showing that stroking an animal is calming and distracts you from your problems.

Talk Positively to Yourself

If you're prone to putting yourself down, you're not alone: behavioral therapists say up to 77 percent of the things we tell ourselves are negative, hurtful, and make us feel worse, rather than better.

Such negative self-talk is deadly to your energy level, and counterproductive to your efforts to be more of an optimist. (If you remember back to chapter 2, optimists tend to have high levels of pep; pessimists, low levels.)

You can, however, put an end to constant self-criticism by replacing it with positive self-talk, suggests Shad Helmstetter, Ph.D., founder of the Self-Talk Institute in Tucson, Arizona, and author of *Self-Talk for Weight Loss*.

According to Dr. Helmstetter, neurological research shows that negative messages create actual physical pathways in the brain. The more you put yourself down, the stronger the physical pathways in your brain become.

The only way to change old self-critical messages is to replace them with new messages—and create new pathways, Dr. Helmstetter says. Starve the old highways by not using them, and that will

Other Ways to Cultivate Optimism

- **Be friendly.** Having positive encounters with others will make you feel good about yourself and the world. As the song goes, "Smile, and the whole world smiles with you."

- **Shrug off bad behavior.** If someone cuts your car off on the highway or slams a door in your face, chalk it up to their bad day and drop it. Don't seek revenge and certainly don't stew on it. That's simply counterproductive.

- **Ban the snowball effect.** In the popular self-help book, *Don't Sweat the Small Stuff—and It's All Small Stuff,* psychologist Richard Carlson advises against allowing negative thoughts to career out of control, throwing you from one bad thought to another, until a snowball has become a mountain of snow. To stop snowballing, pay attention to your thinking and when you catch yourself getting all wound up, just stop the thought—and think of something more positive.

- **Approach new tasks with a can-do, positive self-talking attitude.** Remember the children's book *The Little Engine That Could*? Well, if you think you can, think you can, think you can—you can.

- **Emphasize the fun side of life.** When life gives you lemons, turn them into lemonade. (Clichés and platitudes may be commonplace, but they were designed for a good reason: to remind us of what's really important in life.) Distract yourself from bad events, look for opportunities to laugh, and let the child in you have a field day.

deprive them of the chemicals they need to sustain themselves and cause them to break down.

To begin reprogramming, start by spending a few days listening in on your conversations with yourself and others. For instance, if you're trying to lose weight and failing miserably, you might find that you've been telling yourself that "diet plans don't work, so why bother?" or "I'm not sticking to my diet anyway, so one little chocolate bar won't hurt me"——messages that set you up for failure.

Next, replace the negative thoughts with positive messages: "I'll only eat healthy, nutritious foods today"; "I'm going to take care of myself."

Don't be discouraged if it takes a few weeks for self-talk to take hold; research shows that it can take three months or longer to create new positive self-talk pathways. "With repetition, you'll start to develop new messages that will become as unconscious and automatic as the old messages," Dr. Helmstetter assures.

Esther Bogin, M.S., C.C.C., of People Communication Skills in Long Island, New York, suggests these techniques for more positive self-talk:

• **Use the 2:1 ratio:** Catch yourself doing something right twice as often as you catch yourself doing something wrong.

• **Use active, positive language when talking to yourself.** Say "I can, I will, I am . . ."

• **Make an audiotape with a positive message for yourself.** "Most of our self-talk is unconscious," says Bogin, "so play the tape while you're relaxing or sleeping so it will sink into your brain."

Positive self-talk can also be used for building self-esteem, improving athletic performance, in business, and in personal relationships.

So what's next? In chapter 7, we'll look into the value of vitamins, minerals, and herbs in boosting energy. These products aren't panaceas for an energy lag, but they can be a helpful part of an overall pep-boosting regimen.

THE BOTTOM LINE

A number of lifestyle changes can lead to an increase in zip. Topping the list are good sleep habits (keeping a regular sleep-wake schedule and getting enough rest). Losing weight, stopping smoking, consuming alcohol only in moderation, and taking frequent work and vacation breaks are also important.

Other strategies include learning and using relaxation techniques daily, managing your time better and getting organized, adopting a more positive attitude, and developing interests and hobbies that make you feel good about yourself and your life.

....

Vitamin, Mineral, and Herbal Supplements

Our bodies need vitamins and minerals to survive—and to produce energy. While most experts would like you to get these nutrients from foods, dietary supplements are now a staple of the American diet. They're also a $12 billion industry. Benjamin Caballero, M.D., Ph.D., director of the Johns Hopkins Center for Human Nutrition, reports in *The Johns Hopkins Health Insider* that half of Americans take a multivitamin as extra insurance against a poor diet. Many also take antioxidants—vitamins C, E, and beta carotene—to ward off heart disease, cancer, and other ailments, as well as various "nutriceuticals" (herbs and the like). Amino acids, enzymes, hormones, and other natural products are also making their way into the spotlight and are being touted as anti-aging, energy-boosting, miracle cures.

What Do Vitamins and Minerals Do?

Vitamins are organic substances that the body requires to perform a myriad of functions. They typically come from plant foods and supplements.

There are actually two categories of vitamins: water-soluble vitamins such as the B and C vitamins, which are easily dissolvable in water; and fat-soluble vitamins such as A, D, E, and K, which must be combined with bile acids before they can be dissolved and absorbed into the bloodstream. Water-soluble vitamins quickly pass through the body; the body uses what it needs and excretes the rest. Fat-soluble vitamins, on the other hand, can accumulate in the liver and fat tissue, which makes them more dangerous if they're overconsumed.

Minerals—calcium, potassium, zinc, magnesium, iron, iodine, and the others—are also critical to many bodily functions. They are classified as inorganic substances because they do not contain carbon, as vitamins do. Humans typically ingest their minerals in the form of plant and animal products, and by taking supplements.

The Value of B Vitamins

In terms of energy, there are no more important vitamins than those in the B category: these are the catalysts that help your body convert carbohydrates, protein, and fat into energy. For instance, thiamin (B_1), riboflavin (B_2), and niacin (B_3) help produce energy in all the cells of your body. Deficiencies of these vitamins can therefore cause fatigue, anemia, and other problems.

The B vitamins are so critical to good health that even the the National Academy of Sciences' Food and Nutrition Board—long the stalwart supporter of a diet-only approach to getting vitamins and minerals—is now recommending supplements for some of them. Still, it continues to be important to try to get most B vitamins from your diet, in the form of fruits, vegetables, fortified grain and cereal products, soybeans, milk, eggs, poultry, meat, and fish.

SMART DEFINITION

Dietary supplements

The Food and Drug Administration's definition of dietary supplements encompasses vitamins, minerals, proteins, amino acids, botanicals (including herbs), garlic extract, fish oils, fiber, enzymes, animal extracts, and bioflavonoids. A supplement is intended for ingestion in pill, capsule, tablet, or liquid form, and isn't marketed for use as a conventional food or as the sole item in a meal or diet.

Vitamin Pros and Cons for Healthy People

Vitamin	What It Does	Any Concerns about It?
A/Beta carotene (metabolized into vitamin A in the body)	Needed for growth and reproduction. Helps preserve bones, teeth, skin, eyes, vision, and mucous membranes. Being studied for its antioxidant effects. May help prevent cancer and heart disease.	Vitamin A can be toxic if over-consumed. Beta-carotene is nontoxic but may turn your skin yellow.
B_1 (Thiamin)	B vitamins help to release energy from food sources. They also maintain the brain and nerves, and help in the development of red blood cells.	Doses over 500 mg. can cause itching, tingling, and pain.
B_2 (Riboflavin)		May turn urine orange-yellow.
B_3 (Niacin)		High doses can be toxic.
B_6 (Pyroxidine)		More than 200 mg. a day may produce numbness and other nerve problems.
B_{12}		Believed to be generally nontoxic.
Folate	Needed for creation of DNA; prevents certain types of birth defects when taken during pregnancy. Along with vitamin B_6 may help reduce risk of heart disease by lowering levels of homocysteine. May fight some cancers, too.	Believed to be generally nontoxic.

Vitamin	What It Does	Any Concerns about It?
C	Maintains gums, teeth, bones, and connective tissue, helps heal wounds, and promotes absorption of iron. Being studied as an antioxidant to determine if it can prevent cancer and heart disease.	Large doses may cause diarrhea and kidney stones.
D	Maintains bones and teeth, and helps the body use calcium to ward off osteoporosis.	Toxic in high doses.
E	Assists the body in creating red blood cells and using vitamin K. Shelters body cells from damage. Being studied for its antioxidant effects in fighting heart disease and cancer.	High doses may cause diarrhea, headache, nausea, fatigue, and other problems.
K	Helps blood clot.	Believed to be generally nontoxic.

Iron and Energy

Most people know that iron-poor blood adds up to fatigue. But did you also know that iron deficiency is the most common type of nutritional deficit in the United States and around the world?

Good dietary sources of iron include red meats, grains, and iron-fortified cereals. If your doctor advises you to take supplements (and you should never take supplements without medical advice), consume them with citrus juices or vitamin C to enhance absorption. (For more information on iron, see chapter 3.)

To Supplement or Not to Supplement?

Many nutrition experts and the American Dietetic Association don't believe that most Americans need vitamin and mineral supplements. They say a well-balanced diet should provide all the nutrients required to maintain good health and provide zip. So why are so many people supplementing anyway?

They're looking for a magic pill—that's one reason. Another is that they're trying to compensate for the lack of a healthy, well-balanced diet they're supposed to be getting but aren't. Reports continually suggest that most Americans don't eat the recommended number of servings of fruits and vegetables; most are not even close, which in turn means they may not be getting their full recommended daily allowances (RDAs), either. For instance, the Eating in America II Survey, conducted by MRCA Information Services in 1994 for the National Live Stock and Meat Board, found that men and women are eating about two servings of vegetables a day—compared to the recommended three to five—and two servings of fruit—compared to the recommended two to four.

Most experts won't quibble if you opt for a multivitamin/mineral product that meets the RDAs for most nutrients. Many even stand behind the need for individual supplements of antioxidants such as vitamins E and C, since there's now good, though inconclusive, data that these vitamins will help to prevent heart disease and cancer. (Besides which, vitamin E isn't easy to get from foods.)

Beyond that, you may be risking your health if you take singular supplements. "Large doses of one vitamin or mineral can throw other vitamin/mineral levels out of balance in the body," says Connie Diekman, R.D., a St. Louis dietitian and spokesperson for the American Dietetic Association. And certain vitamins and minerals can be toxic on their own. You may not even realize how much of a particular vitamin or mineral you're getting from foods and supplements, a dangerous scenario when it comes to fat-soluble nutrients such as vitamins A and D.

SMART SOURCES

If you're looking for dietary supplements at a discount, surf to VitaSave's page at www.VitaSave.com. National brand names are 30 to 50 percent off retail prices. Another plus: you can download information about supplement studies.

Instant Energy?

Contrary to the quick-fix hopes of many, vitamin and mineral supplements don't supply immediate energy. "They can't, because energy comes from calories, and vitamins and minerals don't contain any calories," explains Connie Diekman. Usually you'll only notice a difference in your energy level after supplementing if you're very deficient in a particular nutrient.

Current RDAs for Vitamins and Minerals

The RDAs were designed to guide you in getting an average, safe, and adequate amount of the various nutrients your body needs to stay healthy and protect against nutritional deficiencies (scurvy and rickets, for example).

In recent years, the government has begun to update the RDAs and replace them with more specific guidelines called Dietary Reference Intakes (DRIs) (see chart below). So far, only DRIs for calcium, phosphorus, magnesium, vitamin D, fluoride, choline, and the B vitamins have been developed, but eventually all vitamins and minerals represented by the RDAs will be covered (and other recently recognized nutrients may be added to the list).

RDA/DRI Ranges for Adults for Energy-Associated B Vitamins

Thiamin (Vitamin B$_1$)	1.1 mg a day for women, 1.2 mg. a day for men
Riboflavin (Vitamin B$_2$)	1.1 mg a day for women, 1.3 mg.a day for men
Niacin (Vitamin B$_3$)	14 mg a day for women, 16 mg. a day for men
Vitamin B$_6$	1.3 mg. a day
Folate	400 mcg. a day
Vitamin B$_{12}$	2.4 mcg. a day

Source: Institute of Medicine, National Academy of Sciences, 1998

Sorting through Supplement Claims

Purchasing supplements almost requires a Ph.D.: there are so many claims, so much hype, and so little standardization. Here are some clues to what you can live without, according to Joseph A. Romano, Pharm.D., coauthor of *The Vitamin Book*:

Synthetic versus Natural Supplements: There's no qualitative difference between most synthetic and natural vitamins. The disparity is in the price, with natural supplements costing a lot more. Opt for the synthetics, except when it comes to vitamin E, which you should purchase in the more potent natural form.

Brand Name versus Generic Vitamins: Likewise, there's little difference in quality between brand name and generic vitamins that contain the same ingredients. In fact, many chains make their own "me-too" supplements that mimic national brands but are less expensive. Purchase the cheapest brand or generic you can find.

Time-Release Vitamins: Claims that vitamins are time-released and therefore provide more vitamin for your money aren't substantiated by scientific evidence. Actually, the converse may be true: the pill coating may make it more difficult for the body to absorb fat-soluble vitamins. Don't bother with these formulations.

Colloidal Minerals: These expensive products are mineral-rich clays that are suspended in liquid. They're supposed to provide more minerals than the typical pill supplement and they're often touted as cure-alls. Unfortunately, there's no evidence to back up the claims. And some colloidal products have dangerous concentrations of aluminum or other minerals. Avoid them.

Chelated Minerals: These are minerals that are attached to an amino acid. Manufacturers claim they're absorbed more quickly and completely in the body than are nonchelated minerals, but since minerals are separated from the amino acids upon digestion, chelation doesn't actually improve absorption. In fact, *The Berkeley Wellness Letter* says chelated minerals may be less well absorbed than other mineral formulations. Again, the recommendation is to pass them by.

SMART SOURCES

For more information on the RDAs and DRIs, visit the National Academy of Science's Web site at www.nas.edu.

Why change to DRIs? Because reams of research now shows how important vitamins and minerals can be in not only warding off deficiency diseases, but also in reducing the risk of other disorders such as heart disease, diabetes, osteoporosis, and cancer. The DRIs address these issues in a way the RDAs didn't. In addition, the DRIs are needed because they take into account nutrient intake from sources other than regular foods (whereas the RDAs strictly focused on nonenriched food intake). Since so many of us today are supplementing and eating vitamin- and mineral-fortified foods, there's a chance that we could overdose on certain vitamins and minerals; thus, the DRIs stipulate suggested intake levels from all nutrient sources, and oftentimes provide maximum tolerable levels (beyond which side effects are likely to occur).

Herbs and Other Dietary Supplements

A number of herbs, amino acids, and other dietary supplements have been touted for their energy-boosting effects, and are making their way into the mainstream. In fact, they've created outright crazes, selling off the shelves faster than manufacturers can stock them. From melatonin to DHEA, chromium to creatine, Americans are embracing supplements in a big way, making for big business—and leaving lots of room for misinformation, poor-quality products, and outright scams.

According to *USA Today*, about 60 million Americans have tried herbs and other botanicals and some 50 million Americans are currently using these products. The top sellers are echinacea (for colds), ginseng (for energy and warding off the effects of stress), garlic (for lowering cholesterol), gingko biloba (for improving circulation to the brain and memory), and St. John's wort (for relieving mild to moderate depression).

Herbs have, of course, been utilized for their healing and restorative properties for hundreds of years and in cultures spanning the globe. But the thing to remember when taking herbs is that while they may often be safer than synthetic drugs, they're not entirely benign. (Natural does not always equal safe.)

Some of the pitfalls associated with taking herbs include:

• Many of their positive and negative effects on the body and mind haven't been well-studied or elucidated.

• You may have a different reaction to an herb, just as to a drug, than another person.

• Herbs may interact with medications you're taking.

• You don't always know what you're getting. Herbal concentrations aren't continuous across all products and vary widely. Your best bet is to look for products that contain standardized extracts, which means that the herb concentration has been tested and quantified so that each dose delivers the same amount.

• You may fall prey to misleading advertising. The FDA has little jurisdiction over supplement claims (unless a product purports to diagnose, prevent,

SMART SOURCES

Food and Drug Administration Center for Food Safety and Applied Nutrition
800-FDA-4010
www.fda.gov

Listen to recorded messages, speak to a public affairs specialist (12 noon–4 P.M. ET weekdays), or report a food- or supplement-related illness; on the Web, surf FDA press releases and other documents.

SMART SOURCES

American Botanical
  Council
P.O. Box 144345
Austin, TX 78714
512-926-4900
800-373-7105 (voice-
  activated order line)
www.herbalgram.org

Request 32-page
catalog for $2.50 or a
one year's subscription
to the quarterly
magazine *HerbalGram*
for $25.

Herb Research
  Foundation
1007 Pearl St., Suite
  200
Boulder, CO 80302
800-748-2617
303-449-2265
www.herbs.org/herbs

For a fee, will provide
information packets on
herbal therapies,
specific herbs or
specific topics (e.g.,
stimulants), and
perform literature
searches. Also offers a
hotline for immediate
answers over the
phone.

treat, or cure a specific disease). As a result of the Dietary Supplement Health and Education Act (DSHEA) of 1994, it's up to supplement manufacturers to ensure the claims they're making about products are accurate. And botanicals don't have to undergo rigorous safety testing the way drugs do before they're put on the market.

"If you're considering taking an herb, I recommend that you find a reputable, trained herbalist who knows something about the products he or she is recommending and can guide you in its use," says Jennifer A. Reynolds, a chiropractor, certified herbalist, and certified clinical nutritionist, as well as proprietor of the Weston Wellness Center and The Herb Shop in Weston, Vermont. "A clerk at a chain health-food store isn't likely to have the training to advise you about safety, quality, and appropriate administration." You can also turn to a physician or pharmacist who has taken herb courses, or a licensed naturopathic physician, who must study botanicals extensively as part of his or her training.

(See chapter 8 for information on herbs and other natural products you shouldn't use because of safety concerns.)

Safe Herb Use

• **Take herbs in moderation.** Start with low doses and don't exceed dosages listed on product labeling or recommended by a certified herbalist or physician.

• **Don't take herbs if you're pregnant or breast feeding.**

• **Buy herbs only from reputable places**—a certified herbablist, health food store, or drugstore. Herbs should be sealed and labeled with the name and location of the manufacturer.

• **Bone up on the pros and cons of herb use.** Don't just trust manufacturers' often-biased information pamphlets; read magazine articles and books on the subject.

• **Take only one herb at a time,** in case you develop side effects. That way you'll know which herb is the culprit.

• **Stop taking an herb if you develop side effects** such as nausea, vomiting, diarrhea, or headache within a couple of hours of taking a dose. If you experience a severe reaction, seek immediate medical attention.

• **Discuss your supplement use with your regular doctor** to ensure you're not taking any medications that could interact dangerously with the herb or other supplement.

Herb Supplement Forms

Herbs come in a variety of forms. Here's a quick guide to herbal tinctures, extracts, decoctions, and infusions:

• **Extracts and tinctures:** These formulations contain herbs in a liquid base. Usually, the herb is infused in alcohol to maintain its potency. (Vinegar, glycerin, or water may also be used.) Take an extract or tincture in a beverage, such as juice or

WHAT MATTERS, WHAT DOESN'T

What Matters
• Good scientific studies that support supplement claims.

• Government recommendations about supplement safety.

• Relying on a certified herbalist or health professional who has researched supplement claims.

• Purchasing only standardized herb products.

What Doesn't
• The latest supplement fad.

• The advice of the clerk at the local chain health food store.

F.Y.I.

Infusions, decoctions, and teas can all taste and/or smell bad, making them unpleasant to drink; try adding honey, sugar, or lemon to make them easier to swallow.

water, or place drops directly under the tongue (the herb will be absorbed faster there).

• **Tablets/capsules:** These formulations contain a concentrated amount of powdered herb, so you get a good dose of herb in an easy-to-ingest, palatable package. Take tablets and capsules with an eight-ounce glass of water to help break down the pill and aid your body in absorbing the herb quickly and fully.

• **Teas, decoctions, and infusions:** These formulations start out as dried herbs that you simmer or steep in boiling or very hot water. You get a tea when you steep dried herbs in boiling water for three to five minutes. You get a decoction when you simmer roots and barks of dried herbs in boiling water for ten to twenty minutes. And you get an infusion when you steep flowers, leaves, and stems of fresh or dried herbs in very hot water for ten to twenty minutes. Decoctions and infusions contain stronger concentrations of herb than do teas.

"I like teas, infusions, and decoctions because they are easily assimilated by the body," says Dr. Reynolds. "Your body needs liquid to absorb the herb, and the hot water helps to further release its medicinal power. In addition, you don't have to burn any energy to release the herbs, the way you do with a capsule or tablet."

"Hot" Supplements

Below is an overview of some of the hottest herbs on the market today, outlining what is known about each, what it is used for, and the pros and cons associated with taking the herb.

Ginseng

Ginseng is the top energy herb. This stimulant has long been used and recommended to increase vitality, mental alertness, physical performance, endurance, and concentration, and to decrease physical fatigue.

Herbalists classify ginseng as an adaptogen or balancer, which means it helps the body to better adapt to internal and external stress. It is also believed to boost immunity to disease.

Ginseng can be used as a quick pick-me-up—in tea, tablet, drop, or capsule form. There are three major types: Asian ginseng (Panax ginseng), American ginseng (Panax quinquefolius), and Siberian ginseng (Eleutherococcus senticosus). American ginseng is typically milder and less stimulating than Asian ginseng; some products contain a mixture of types.

"Some people may feel a noticeable surge in energy after taking one form of ginseng or another," notes Dr. Reynolds. "Others may just notice they're less fatigued. And still others may feel overstimulated. The effect of any herb on the body is very individual, which is why it pays to experiment to find the type that is most effective for you."

Ginseng can also be taken on a

An Herbalist's List of Energy-Boosting Supplements

Interested in boosting energy? Here are Dr. Jennifer Reynolds's picks for herbs and supplements that may be worth a try:

- Bee pollen
- Cayenne (capsicum)
- Chlorophyll
- Ginger
- Ginseng (especially Siberian)
- Kelp
- Licorice root

"When I'm out at night and I find I'm getting tired, I take twenty drops of Siberian ginseng under the tongue or in a glass of water and it gives me a short burst of energy," says Debra, a thirty-nine-year-old administrator of a preschool. "I also sometimes use ginseng when I find I'm slumping after lunch and have an afternoon meeting where I need to be alert."

Debra likes ginseng because its effects are subtle and, unlike caffeine, it's not addictive. "Ginseng gives me a mental sharpness and kind of revs my engine without producing the speedy buzz I get when I drink coffee," she says. "And I can take it in the afternoon without worrying that it will keep me up all night."

regular daily schedule to provide a long-term energy lift. If you decide to do this, however, you should take a one-week break from the herb every three weeks. (That's wise, since the cumulative effects of extended use are unknown.)

Ginseng is not considered to be toxic—although you shouldn't use it if you have high blood pressure or cardiovascular disease. Nor does it seem to have any significant side effects when taken in moderate doses. (Check the label of the product you buy for guidance.) In some people, however, the herb may cause insomnia, nervousness, breast pain, or diarrhea.

Valerian

Valerian isn't an energy booster per se, but it does enhance sleep and decrease anxiety, which is why it's mentioned here.

Dr. Reynolds recommends a cup of valerian tea before bedtime for people who are having trouble sleeping. "It's very safe, doesn't have the narcotic effect of sleeping pills, and won't make you drowsy the next day," she says. "I think valerian is an excellent weapon against stress and nervous tension. It's very quieting and calming." If you don't like the taste of the tea, take the herb in capsule, tablet, or extract form.

Don't use the herb too frequently, though: excessive use of valerian may cause headaches, excitability, or even insomnia.

Chromium

Chromium is a trace mineral that improves the way the body uses insulin, the hormone that helps deliver glucose (sugar) to the muscles to be converted into energy. Proponents claim that more efficient use of insulin will increase fat-burning and build lean muscle, both of which will result in weight loss and an increase in pep.

While chromium may benefit elite athletes and people with diabetes (since it can help normalize blood sugar levels), most experts say the supplement is not worth the expense for other people. (Despite weight-loss claims, you won't lose pounds with this supplement unless you exercise like a fiend.) Instead, try naturally supplementing your chromium intake by increasing your consumption of nonprocessed whole-bran cereals and breads, broccoli, prunes, and chicken breasts. Or take a multivitamin that contains it.

Carnitine

Carnitine is an amino acid that is made in the liver and found in foods such as red meat. It is needed to transport and help break down fat to generate energy. As a supplement, carnitine is touted to improve athletic performance and help with weight loss.

Proponents believe that the more carnitine you have available in the body, the more fat you'll burn—but again, only if you exercise. But studies haven't shown that taking carnitine supplements actually gets the amino acid into the muscle where it will help to burn fat (in other words, the

F.Y.I.

Many herbal extracts—including ginseng products—may contain up to 34 to 50 percent alcohol by volume, according to the Bureau of Alcohol, Tobacco, and Firearms. Some health food stores, such as General Nutrition Centers, now require manufacturers to list alcohol content on supplement labels.

To steam off alcohol from herbal extracts, Dr. Jennifer Reynolds recommends putting your dosage into a quarter-cup of hot water. After a few minutes, you can drink the alcohol-free, herb-potent warm water.

SMART MOVE

Herbal energizers are
making their way into
our snack foods and
sodas. For instance,
the antidepressant
herb St. John's wort
(hypericum) can now
be found in a soft
drink. But are you
getting the herbal
benefit you're seeking?
No, says Varro E. Tyler,
Ph.D., Sc.D., and
considered by many to
be America's top
herbalist.

"No matter what the
herb is—St. John's
wort, gingko, echi-
nachea, gotu kola,
yohimbe—adding it to
a food or beverage is
usually just a mar-
keting gimmick," he
writes in his *Prevention*
magazine column "Ask
the Honest Herbalist."
The reason: the dose
is probably too small to
be of benefit (although
it's also unlikely to
hurt you).

body doesn't recognize the supplements as carnitine). "There is also no evidence that carnitine
will enhance athletic performance," says Matthew
Vukovich, Ph.D., assistant professor of exercise science at Wichita State University, Wichita, Kansas.
"Nor does it appear that most people are deficient
in the amino acid."

In addition, at extremely high doses—six
grams a day, which is two to four more grams than
used in most studies—carnitine may produce diarrhea.

Coenzyme Q-10

Coenzyme Q-10 is an antioxidant—meaning it
reverses or prevents damage to cells. It works like
a vitamin and plays a role in breaking down food
and burning oxygen to give cells energy. Researchers are just beginning to study this com-
pound (which we produce naturally in the body),
and much remains to be learned about it.

"There's no evidence that supplements of
coenzyme Q-10 are needed, since most people
don't seem to be deficient in it," says American
Dietetic Association spokesperson Tammy Baker,
R.D. "However, there don't appear to be any side
effects to using it."

If you'd like to naturally boost your production of coenzyme Q-10, eat more mackerel, sar-
dines, and other fatty fish, beef, soy oil, and peanuts.
You can also take vitamin E, B complex, and sele-
nium supplements, all of which encourage the body
to produce the vitamin.

Creatine

Creatine is a popular amino acid supplement that appears to improve athletic performance by providing short bursts of high energy and a temporary increase in muscle strength—say if you're lifting weights or running sprints on the track. *USA Today* says it is second only to vitamins and minerals in popularity among athletes and sells to the tune of some $100 million a year.

That's the good news. The bad news is that its pluses and minuses aren't all known, since it hasn't been studied a great deal, especially over the long term. (Many studies are in the works, however.) The FDA has cautioned people not to take the supplement without consulting a doctor first.

Melatonin

Melatonin is a potent hormone that is made in the body and governs your sleep-wake clock. Production of the hormone declines as you age, and drops sharply after age forty-five.

Melatonin is released by the pineal gland, a tiny structure in the brain. It is produced only in darkness (when the light hitting your eyes fades). When it is sent into the bloodstream, it tells the body that it is night and time to sleep. When light again emerges, melatonin production ceases, which prompts you to wake up.

The hormone has been highly publicized as a natural, effective, and cheap sleep aid as well as a cure for jet lag—and there's actually some data to back up these assertions. Researchers have found that taking melatonin can reset the body's inter-

F.Y.I.

A study published in the *New England Journal of Medicine* in 1993 found that one in three Americans has tried an alternative medical therapy—the majority of them without telling their primary care doctor.

It's important to share information with your physician about the alternative methods you're trying since they may conflict, sometimes dangerously, with traditional therapies. (The herb gingko biloba thins the blood, for instance, and if you take it with aspirin, you might experience excessive bleeding.) Pay close attention to any changes in how you feel when you start on a new therapy; if you experience any unusual sensations such as headache, nausea, or allergy symptoms, stop taking the product and report the problem to your doctor.

nal clock and produce sleep; depending on the time and dose you take, you can push your sleep cycle forward or back in time.

Studies also show that it may reduce jet lag, helping you to sleep better in a new destination and helping to reduce daytime fatigue. The problem is determining the correct dose and time to take melatonin. Ingesting the hormone at the wrong time or in the wrong dose could conceivably make sleep problems and jet lag worse instead of better.

Since much remains to be discovered about melatonin, the government's National Institute on Aging has warned consumers not to take supplements at this time. After all, this is a potent substance made by your body—and supplementing with it could screw up your natural production. And you certainly shouldn't take it on a long-term or daily basis.

In fact, instead of taking a supplement at all, try boosting your body's natural production of melatonin by going to bed on a regular schedule and not drinking alcohol before sleep.

DHEA

Like melatonin, DHEA (dehydroepiandrosterone) is a potent hormone naturally made by the body. After it is produced, it is converted into the female and male sex hormones estrogen and testosterone, as well as into other hormones.

Also like melatonin, DHEA production begins to decline in middle age, which has led some people to suggest that taking replacement doses might prevent problems of aging, such as cancer. Besides being a potential avenue to renewed vitality and vigor, the hormone is said to improve immunity and bolster muscle and bone.

While there is some promising evidence that DHEA may be at least a partial antidote to aging, the National Institute on Aging has cautioned against its use for now. There's cause for concern, too: In high doses, DHEA can cause liver damage, and may be associated with an increased risk for breast and prostate cancers. It may also change the composition of cholesterol in your blood, increasing the risk for heart disease.

Ultimately, like melatonin, it's unwise to supplement a hormone that your body naturally makes, and whose production naturally declines with age, until far more is known about how and why it works.

In chapter 8, we'll review additional alternative routes to energy production. Many of these are scientifically untested, or out-of-the-mainstream techniques that work well for some people. We'll also discuss energy "boosts to beware"—remedies that may do you more harm than good.

THE BOTTOM LINE

Vitality can't be found in a bottle. Vitamins, minerals, herbs, and other dietary supplements aren't magic bullets that can whip your energy level into shape. If you're very deficient in a nutrient, especially one of the energy-essential B vitamins, you might feel a surge if you start to take supplements. If you're not deficient, however, it's unlikely you'll derive any noticeable energy effect.

Likewise, while herbs and other supplements such as creatine, DHEA, and melatonin are now popular, they shouldn't be used in a cavalier manner. Many haven't been studied adequately, and much remains to be learned about their benefits and risks. The safest herb to use to boost energy appears to be ginseng; valerian appears to be a safe sleep aid.

CHAPTER 8

Alternative Energy Fixes

THE KEYS

• Alternative remedies may play an important role in boosting your energy.

• Possibilities include essential oils, flower essences, color therapy, and reflexology.

• Despite many strategies that enhance your energy, there exist "boosts to beware"—herbal practices to avoid.

• Arm yourself with a list of herbs the FDA considers dangerous.

• Learn how to evaluate claims made about supplements.

The topic of energy is a soft one scientifically. There aren't many clinical studies to back up claims that this approach or that one increases pep. And energy is a very individual thing: what may boost your vitality may sap another person's. That makes energy a field ripe for alternative, new-agey, and out-there fixes—not that, in theory, there's anything wrong with such approaches. Indeed, you may want to experiment with a variety of these techniques. Just don't take claims unsupported by scientific data (such as energy guarantees) too seriously, don't overdo any remedy, and stick to remedies that appear to be safe.

Essential Oils and Aromatherapy

Essential oils are oils that are extracted from plants—the blossoms, leaves, and roots—that have a distinct and oftentimes pleasant odor. The oils can be:

• Infused into the air via a device or candle

• Placed on a handkerchief and sniffed

• Massaged into the skin

• Placed on a wet cloth and used as a compress

• Watered down and misted onto the skin

• Poured into a foot or body bath

Several essential oils are believed to increase energy and reduce fatigue and stress. The thinking behind belief in their effects is actually grounded in science. Smell signals move through the olfactory (smell) system to the region of the brain where our emotions and memories are stored. Hence, smells can elicit memories and feelings. You have likely experienced this phenomenon yourself many times: the odor of bread baking, for instance, may remind you of your grandmother, who used to make a loaf from scratch on holidays. A certain cologne may remind you of an old flame. The smell of a wet dog may remind you of a puppy you once had.

If you're interested in using essential oils, follow these tips culled from *500 Formulas for Aromatherapy: Mixing Essential Oils for Every Use,* by Carol and David Schiller:

• Always "water down" highly concentrated essential oils in sweet almond, grapeseed, flaxseed, or sesame oil (the latter are called carrier oils). Recipes vary depending on the oils used, but typically you put several drops of the essential oil into several teaspoons or a tablespoon of carrier oil.

• Avoid getting oils or their vapors in or around your eyes.

• Don't drink alcohol when using essential oils.

• Don't ingest essential oils.

• If you're pregnant, breast feeding, or highly allergic, avoid use of essential oils.

SMART SOURCES

Natura Essentials
27134A Paseo
  Espada, Suite 323
San Juan Capistrano,
  CA 92675
800-933-1008

Sells quality essential
oils, candles, and
aromatherapy devices.

National Association
  for Holistic Aroma-
  therapy
219 Carl Street
San Francisco, CA
  94117
415-564-6785

Sells quality essential
oils.

Oils for Alertness

Here are some oils that Schiller and Schiller say are energizing:

- Cumin

- Ginger

- Grapefruit

- Juniper berries

- Lemon

- Lime

- Peppermint

- Pine

- Rosemary

- Spearmint

Where to Obtain Oils

Essential oils are fairly easy to find: Many new age stores sell them, as do some gift shops and department stores. You can also get them via mail order (look in new age and alternative health magazines for company names and in the "Smart Sources" sidebar on this page).

Schiller and Schiller recommend buying only high-quality, 100-percent-pure oils, despite the fact that they can be expensive. Look for unrefined carrier oils, and essential oils that have been extracted from the plants via steam distillation, mechanical pressing, or by an expeller. (Inferior oils are made of synthetic substances or extracted with chemical solvents, which can affect their ability to produce the desired effects.)

Flower Essences

The theory and use of flower essences—ingestion of a concoction of flower extracts to change your mood—was first developed in the 1930s by an English physician named Dr. Edward Bach.

When you consume a few drops of the liquid that is extracted from a flower, the essence is believed to vibrate through your body, creating harmony. It sounds hokey, but many mainstream physicians and nurses who are favorably inclined toward alternative medicine have seen flower essences work for their patients.

"The great thing about flower essences is they are inexpensive, nontoxic, and nonaddictive," says Susan Cohen, R.N., Ph.D., a Lynbrook, New York, clinical specialist in psychiatric and mental health.

Typically, you take two drops of an essence (which has no taste) in spring water four times a day. Oftentimes, essences are mixed together to create a variety of effects and to counter specific mood problems (for instance, you might take lavender to soothe your nerves, along with mustard to relieve feelings of glumness, and California Wild Rose to imbue you with enthusiasm). However, Dr. Cohen advises against mixing more than six different essences in one combination.

SMART MOVE

Don't be duped by patient testimonials (anecdotes about how a remedy helped someone). Oftentimes, these testimonials hide a lack of scientific data about a product. And just because someone else says a product or service worked for them, doesn't mean it will work for you.

Also look askance on claims that a product is a quick and easy solution to your energy problem. If a product makes claims that seem too good to be true or guarantees results, it's probably not to be trusted, says Connie Diekman, R.D.

Approach all unproven therapies—as well as most alternative practitioners—with a healthy dose of skepticism.

SMART SOURCES

Flower Essence Society
Earth-Spirit, Inc.
P.O. Box 459
Nevada City, CA 95959
800-548-0075
(Monday–Thursday
   8 A.M.–3:30 P.M. PT)

Request educational materials and class schedules, purchase their book *The Flower Essence Repertory*, get referrals to practitioners, and purchase essences.

"You can't fix everything at once," she says. She also recommends giving an essence a couple of weeks to work; it can take that long for an effect to take hold. (As with essential oils, however, if you're highly allergic, pregnant, or breast feeding, don't try flower essences.)

Flower Essences That Boost Energy

The Flower Essence Repertory by Patricia Kaminski and Richard Katz, recommends the following essences for boosting energy:

- Blackberry

- California Wild Rose

- Cayenne

- Hornbeam

- Morning glory

- Nasturtium

- Peppermint

Where to Purchase Essences

You can obtain flower essences from the Flower Essence Society or from health food stores and alternative health catalogs for about $6 to $8 a bottle. The big question, though, is which ones to take, since there are so many. The Society can refer you to practitioners who will prescribe specific essences for you, or you can design your own special blend.

Color Therapy

Many cultures have used color to create energy and treat a variety of ills. There is even some evidence that certain colors help to calm or energize by synchronizing different areas of the brain. There's certainly no harm associated with experimenting with color to increase energy. So feel free to use color therapy in your home, your clothing, or your car.

Although color effects are highly individualized, here are some commonly accepted associations:

• **Red:** Physically activating and energizing. It is associated with passion.

• **Yellow:** Mentally stimulating and cheerful.

• **Orange:** Refreshing.

• **Green:** Calming and soothing and believed to counteract stress. (That's why it's a favored color for hospital wards.)

• **Blue:** Relaxing, but less so than green.

• **Violet:** Can help with sleep.

SMART SOURCES

International Institute
    of Reflexology
P.O. Box 12642
St. Petersburg, FL
    33733-2642
727-343-4811

Request a referral to a
certified reflexologist in
your area and educa-
tional materials for
consumers.

American Academy of
    Reflexology
606 E. Magnolia, #B
Burbank, CA 91501
818-841-7741

Request consumer
information.

Reflexology

This foot therapy is based on the ancient Asian principle of chi—the energy force that flows through the body. (When chi is blocked, imbalance occurs and you may suffer fatigue or other symptoms.) Whether you believe in chi or not, most people say that reflexology is relaxing and helps reduce tension.

Reflexology practitioners believe that there are ten energy zones in the body. All of these zones can be manipulated and brought into balance by massaging and then pressing on certain parts of the foot.

Some specific sites and their correlations include:

• The toes = the head.

• The base of the toes = the neck.

• The balls of the feet = the lungs, breasts, heart, and chest.

• The underside of the midfoot = the diaphragm and upper abdominal organs.

• The heel = the pelvic area.

• The bone along the arch of the foot = the spine.

• The top of the foot = the back.

• The top of the foot near the ankle = reproductive organs.

If you'd like to try reflexology, look for an experienced practitioner who has been certified by the International Institute of Reflexology (see sidebar). You want to be sure you're getting the real thing, and not just a glorified foot massage from an untrained pedicurist or masseuse.

Boosts to Beware

Here are some other popular remedies that are considered hazardous or potentially hazardous when used to boost energy.

Ephedra (Ma Huang)

This Chinese herb and amphetamine-like stimulant can be found in many natural energy, bodybuilding, and diet aids. It's been linked with several deaths when taken in large doses. It is currently on the FDA's list of hazardous herbs because it can lead to dizziness, headaches, stomach upset, heart palpitations, a rise in blood pressure, a fast heartbeat, heart attacks, and seizures.

Natural ephedra energy-boosting products may also contain other stimulants, such as caffeine, which can exacerbate the side effects of the herb. In 1995, the FDA took a diet pill called Nature's Nutrition Formula One, which contained ephedrine (a form of ephedra) and kola nut (a caffeinelike ingredient), off the market because it had received over one hundred reports of serious adverse effects associated with the product, including heart attacks, headaches, and several deaths.

In 1996, the FDA warned consumers not to purchase or consume dietary supplements containing ephedrine to boost mood, or as an alternative to

SMART DEFINITION

Ma huang (or ephedra)

A Chinese herb that contains a number of compounds. Most prominent is ephedrine, a cardiac stimulant, that is also often found in decongestant medications.

the illegal street drug "ecstacy" (a hallucinogenic amphetamine). These products are being marketed as legal highs, and claim to produce euphoria, increased sexual sensation, heightened awareness, and increased energy. "The ingredient panels on these products may list ma huang, Chinese ephedra, ma huang extract, ephedra, Ephedra sinica, ephedra extract, ephedra herb powder, epitonin, or ephedrine," the FDA stated. "Any one of these ingredients listed on the label indicates the presence of ephedrine in the product."

Given its potential for side effects, it's best to avoid ephedra. If you do use it, don't take more than eight milligrams in a six-hour period or twenty-four milligrams a day, or use it for longer than seven days at a time. ("Long-term intake increases the risk of serious side effects," says the FDA.) Be sure to avoid ephedra if you have high blood pressure, kidney disease, diabetes, a malfunctioning thyroid gland, or heart disease.

Super Blue-Green Algae

You may have heard that blue-green algae are great energy boosters. However, not all algae are alike; one—alphanizomenon flos-aquae (AFA)—may even be dangerous.

AFA is harvested from a single source—Klamath Lake in Oregon—and freeze- or flash-dried into pill form. It is most commonly sold as Super Blue-Green Algae and is marketed by distributors nationwide via a pyramid system (where users become sellers of the product in an effort to keep their costs down). A two- to four-month supply costs over $100, according to manufacturer Cell-Tech.

There are scores of devotees of AFA around

the United States who claim that the algae brings them supernatural energy, and relief from various ailments. But there are scientists, nutritionists, and others who doubt these claims and worry that AFA is coming from a polluted lake and is more like expensive pond scum than health food.

Manufacturers say that the unique environmental conditions of Klamath Lake combine to make AFA one of the most nutrient-dense foods available to man. Their nutritional analyses indicate the algae contains a full spectrum of vitamins and minerals, chorophyll, high amounts of protein, some carbohydrates, and fiber.

Mainstream nutritionists who have reviewed AFA literature put out by manufacturers say that we don't need as much protein as AFA supplies, and that all the claims about the product are based on user testimonials and anecdotes, rather than on scientifically rigorous studies. They're also concerned about the lethargy, nausea, diarrhea, headache, and skin breakouts that some people experience when they first begin using AFA. "That sounds like a mild case of food poisoning to me," says Tammy Baker, R.D., an American Dietetic Association spokesperson. Cell-Tech distributors call this a "detoxification effect" or a "cleansing process," and say it can be averted by taking probiotics, such as acidophilus and bifidus, and enzymes along with the algae. But nutritionists fire back that the body doesn't need to detoxify through the ingestion of outside materials and that the described symptoms are worrisome. "Detoxification is the job of the liver, not of algae," says Baker.

Given the lack of data, and the potential that the algae is coming from a polluted lake and is expensive, it makes better sense to spend your money on good nutrition rather than on AFA.

F.Y.I.

The government has relatively little control over dietary supplement manufacturers and what they put on the market. Manufacturers are trusted to put out safe products, with truthful claims. It's only when consumers, doctors, or groups make reports to the FDA that a product is unsafe or is being touted to prevent or cure a health problem (such as cancer), that the agency can look into taking it off the market.

If you experience an adverse effect after taking a dietary supplement, call and report it to the FDA at 800-FDA-4010. If enough calls are logged about a specific product, the FDA can take steps to remove it from the market.

A retired real estate agent, Barbara, sixty-eight, is open to new and natural therapies and thus was agreeable to trying kombucha tea.

"My daughter told me about kombucha and was able to get a starter 'mushroom' from a friend for me," she recalls. "It took a lot of work to ferment and make the tea, but I thought the effort might be worth it if it boosted my energy level or helped my health. Unfortunately, the mushroom didn't do anything for me."

Fortunately, it didn't harm her either. Barbara discontinued drinking the tea after a month when she heard on the news that it had been associated with some ill effects. "I'm not sorry I tried it," she says, "and I'm still open to alternative remedies, but I'll be a little more cautious next time."

Kombucha Tea

Kombucha (pronounced calm-boo-sha) mushroom tea is a cure-all that swept the nation a couple of years ago. It's supposed to enhance energy; improve digestion and metabolism; boost the immune system; reduce inflammation; reverse the course of AIDS, multiple sclerosis, and cancer; shrink the prostate; relieve arthritis, psoriasis, wrinkles, baldness, premenstrual syndrome, and acne; spur weight loss; and improve memory. At one time, it was believed that as many as 3 to 6 million people were drinking the sour, ciderlike tea—and not only health-conscious types in California and New York, but people in regions as diverse as Iowa, Florida, and Arizona.

Actually, the kombucha mushroom isn't really a mushroom, but a mixture of yeast and bacteria—a slippery, rubbery-looking, brownish pancake that is floated in a tea-and-sugar liquid at room temperature to form a fermented drink. You brew and ferment the tea yourself after you receive a kombucha "mother" from an enthusiastic acquaintance or purchase one from a commercial distributor. You can also buy the liquid alone at health food stores.

While the claims about kombucha all sound well and good, there's little scientific evidence to support them. What's more, the tea may be dangerous: there's already been one death in Iowa that may be related to the tea (although the link is tenuous and unconfirmed). And reported side effects of the tea include stomach upset, overstimulation (thanks to its caffeine), sores in the mouth, and yeast infections.

The concern is that people trying to culture kombucha at home may not be doing so under sterile conditions and the "mushroom" may get contaminated with microorganisms such as *Aspergillus,* which can be deadly. Some experts believe the tea may be especially dangerous for people with allergies to antibiotics and sensitivities to microorganisms, such as those who are immunocompromised.

Because of the unknowns associated with kombucha, most medical experts say it is best to avoid the brew.

How to Evaluate Supplement Studies and Claims

With new studies coming out daily and being widely reported in the press, it can be difficult to separate the research wheat from the chaff. Here are some criteria you can use to evaluate how good a new study may be—and whether its findings are worth following:

• **Look at who did the research** and where it's published. It's not unusual for a company to sponsor research about its own product—if they don't, who will?—but then you need to take the results with a grain of salt. Look for studies performed at well-known universities and research centers, and published in respected journals, such as the *New England Journal of Medicine, The Lancet,* or the *Journal of*

Dangerous Herbs

The Food and Drug Administration (FDA) considers the following herbs dangerous to human health:

- Chaparral *(Larrea tridentata)*
- Comfrey *(Symphytum officinale)*
- Lobelia *(Lobelia inflata)*
- Germander *(Teucrium* genus)
- Willow bark *(Salix* species)
- Herbal products containing *Stephania* and *Magnolia* species
- Ma huang (ephedra)
- Wormwood

the American Medical Association. (These are peer-reviewed journals, which means that all articles are read and critiqued by peers of the authors for flaws in methodology and interpretation; the manuscripts are then returned to the authors for revisions prior to publication.)

• **Look at the type of research performed.** The best type of scientific study is the clinical trial, in which patients are randomly designated to receive either the active drug or agent or a placebo in such a way that the participants and the investigators don't know who's getting what until the trial is over. This reduces the potential for bias in interpreting the results.

• **Look for supporting research for any study.** One study does not make a case for taking a supplement or using a therapy. All too often, studies produce conflicting results, so you can't be sure of a therapy's true effects until several studies with similar results have been performed and published.

• **Pay greater attention to studies in humans than animals.** Findings in animals don't always translate to humans. And studies in men don't always apply to women, and vice versa.

• **Look for a large number of study subjects and a long study period.** In general, the greater the number of subjects, and the longer the study, the greater the likelihood the results are trustworthy and not just due to chance or error.

Energy All Day, Every Day

Throughout this book, we've discussed a slew of techniques for enhancing your energy level. At least a few (and hopefully more than a few) of these strategies will work for you.

Overall, the most important thing you can do to boost your pep is to learn about your personal daily energy cycles and plan around them so you can get the most out of every day and every moment.

Also high on the list: respect your body and feed it well, give it the rest it requires, and get your blood pumping with some physical activity.

Don't forget to give your mind a break, too: use both sides of your brain—the logical, orderly left side and the creative, impulsive right side. Engage your mind in challenging tasks and let it relax on a daily basis by performing deep breathing or meditation. When all else fails, go for the "flow": fight boredom by engaging yourself in something you find worthwhile that fills you with pleasure and purpose. It can be a craft, a good novel, a game of chess, play with your dog, or helping others.

Building energy really isn't so hard, but it does take some work. (What in life comes without effort?) But if you build a life you love and you love your life, energy will surely follow.

THE BOTTOM LINE

Alternative energy fixes are abundant. Some are helpful, others are not, and some can be downright dangerous. Health experts say it's okay to try remedies that haven't been associated with ill effects—essential oils, reflexology, and color therapy all fall into that category—since the road to boosting energy level is a highly individual one for each person.

But don't fall victim to fancy marketing schemes or consumer ravings about expensive products. Unsubstantiated claims are the hallmark of scams.

Appendix: Energy Boosts on the Spot

Fuel, exercise, sleep, relaxation, flow—now you have covered the basics. But you still might need to create some zip in a hurry—perhaps when you have a presentation after lunch and you are feeling sluggish, or when you have company coming and you are beat.

When you're dragging your feet, try one or more of these for a boost:

Take a Quick Walk

A brisk ten-minute walk can boost your energy level and mood for up to two hours.

Pet Your Dog or Cat

Studies show contact with animals helps lower your heart rate and blood pressure (their's, too). By relaxing, you'll ultimately get a boost in pep.

Drink a Glass of Water

Dehydration is a primary cause of fatigue.

Have a Piece of Fruit

Go for a banana, an apple, or an orange to quickly get some glucose into your blood.

Drink Juice

A fruit juice's simple sugars give you an immediate kick, and the juice's water will fuel you.

Pour the Caffeine

The old standby: any caffeinated drink—coffee, tea, or cola—should give you a temporary lift.

Munch on a Candy Bar

The sugar rush sure feels fine, but it's only a temporary fix, so watch the calories.

Drop Ginseng under Your Tongue

Follow directions on the ginseng and place several drops under your tongue or in a beverage.

Play Stimulating Music

The right kind of music can be energizing while you work or study. Classical is worth a try.

Squeeze a Stress Ball

Foam balls and medicine balls are designed to release tension; they also induce calm energy.

Have a Laugh

A good one distracts negativity, lowers your stress level, and just makes you feel better.

Simulate a Smile

A bogus smile isn't as intoxicating as a real one, but it stimulates physical relaxation just as well.

Wear Red

It's the color of energy, activity, and passion. Yellow is also stimulating.

Seek the Light

Light influences our sleep-wake cycle. When dragging, spend a half hour near or in the sun.

Splash Your Face

It's one of the oldest tricks in the book, but splashing your face with cold water stimulates blood circulation and awakens your senses.

Take a Power Nap

Fifteen to thirty minutes of rest can revive you for hours. (A long nap will have the opposite effect.)

Do a Relaxation Exercise

Deep breathing, the Relaxation Response, Transcendental Meditation: they all work.

Jump Rope

A fun, easy, but intense exercise that's sure to get your blood pumping.

Vent in Your Diary

Don't be uptight about what you write; let your thoughts and feelings flow freely.

Sniff Peppermint

Peppermint-scented essential oil will clear mental fog and stimulate the brain.

Index

Books in the
Smart Guide™ Series

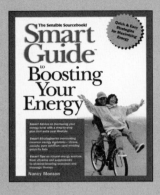

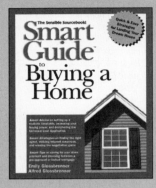

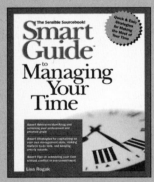

Smart Guide™ to
Boosting Your Energy

Smart Guide™ to
Buying a Home

Smart Guide™ to
Getting Strong and Fit

Smart Guide™ to
Getting Thin and
Healthy

Smart Guide™ to
Healing Foods

Smart Guide™ to
Making Wise
Investments

Smart Guide™ to
Managing Personal
Finance

Smart Guide™ to
Managing Your Time

Smart Guide™ to
Profiting from Mutual
Funds

Smart Guide™ to
Relieving Stress

Smart Guide™ to
Starting a Small Business

Smart Guide™ to
Vitamins and Healing
Supplements

Available soon:

Smart Guide™ to
Healing Back Pain

Smart Guide™ to
Maximizing Your
401(k) Plan

Smart Guide™ to
Planning for Retirement

Smart Guide™ to
Planning Your Estate

Smart Guide™ to
Sports Medicine

Smart Guide™ to
Yoga